Yale College Series, 12

THOMAS HARDY: THE RETURN
OF THE REPRESSED

A Study of the Major Fiction

Perry Meisel

New Haven and London, Yale University Press

YALE PRESS M-1802   B6205   2-27-73   (4)

This volume is number 12 in the Yale College Series
of scholarly essays written by members of the senior
class in Yale College. The series was begun in 1964.

Library of Congress catalog card number: 77–182211
International standard book number: 0–300–01440–6

Designed by John O. C. McCrillis
and set in Baskerville type.
Printed in the United States of America by
The Murray Printing Company,
Forge Village, Massachusetts.

Published in Great Britain, Europe, and Africa by
Yale University Press, Ltd., London. Distributed in Canada by
McGill-Queen's University Press, Montreal; in Latin
America by Kaiman & Polon, Inc., New York City;
in India by UBS Publishers' Distributors Pvt., Ltd., Delhi;
in Japan by John Weatherhill, Inc., Tokyo.

For my parents

Natural selection will modify the structure of the young in relation to the parent, and of the parent in relation to the young. In social animals it will adapt the structure of each individual for the benefit of the community; if each in consequence profits by the selected change.

Darwin, *The Origin of Species*

Contents

Preface

The critical perspective of this book does not necessarily seek the unity of individual works. It attempts instead to define a movement through the entire development of Hardy's major fiction which suggests the historical contours outlined in the introduction. The historical nature of his imaginative explorations is also implied in the occasional references to other writers, especially those who were members of the generation following Hardy's.

The references and allusions to Freud are used simply to consolidate scattered impulses in Hardy, and to provide a conceptual synthesis of the novelist's often vague but important suggestions of still unuttered but implied meanings. Similarly, the use of other novelists aims at an illustration of equally dim, but again central, creative instincts in a structural direction.

This study was originally written as my senior essay in Yale College. Only minor changes and additions have been made. I am especially indebted to my adviser in English, Richard S. Sylvester, whose unfailing guidance and wisdom have been essential to my years at Yale. I am also grateful to my adviser in history, Franklin L. Baumer, and to Edward J. Mendelson, who introduced me to Thomas Hardy. I also wish to thank the 1970 Wrexham Prize committee for initiating the steps toward the publication of the essay.

New Haven
May 1970, March 1971

Textual Note

All page references and citations from Hardy's fiction are from the "Anniversary Edition" of *The Writings of Thomas Hardy* (New York and London: Harper & Brothers, 1940). The following works are used in this study; each entry includes the date of its first appearance in book form:

> *Under the Greenwood Tree, or the Mellstock Quire* (1872)
> *A Pair of Blue Eyes* (1873)
> *Far From the Madding Crowd* (1874)
> *The Return of the Native* (1878)
> *The Life and Death of the Mayor of Casterbridge, a Story of a Man of Character* (1886)
> *The Woodlanders* (1887)
> *Tess of the d'Urbervilles, a Pure Woman Faithfully Presented* (1891)
> *Jude the Obscure* (1896)
> *The Well-Beloved, a Sketch of a Temperament* (1897)

All page references and citations from Florence Emily Hardy, *The Life of Thomas Hardy, 1840–1928* (New York: Macmillan, 1965) are indicated by the abbreviation *Life*. Richard Purdy's *Thomas Hardy: A Bibliographical Study* (1954) has established that the *Life* is "in reality an autobiography," prepared for posthumous publication by Hardy himself (cf. pp. 262–67, 268–73).

References and citations from Hardy's poetry are from the *Collected Poems* (London: Macmillan, 1968).

1   Introduction

Thomas Hardy's novels span a period that saw both the fullness of the Victorian climate and its decline. The primary characteristic of his fiction is tension—a tension that permeates the development of his universe in prose and that lends a distinctly historical aspect to his work. Before Hardy began writing fiction, he had experienced a loss of religious faith and a corresponding conversion to rationalism that was characteristic of not a few young men of the time. His early novels reflect the implications of that first great change in his mental development. Religion also meant belief in a community, the Dorset of his childhood and youth; reason suggested, too, the isolation of the truth-seeking intellect, an urban sensibility that rose in opposition to the rural. By the time he wrote *The Return of the Native,* Hardy had set out to explore the nature of both experiences in their interrelation. From that point on, his novels record a progressively deeper recognition of the latent concern within these initial questions, the isolated individual self-alienated by his own awareness.

Hardy passed his childhood and early youth in the Dorset of his forefathers. His family had a long tradition of participation in the church choir at Stinsford, and while the custom ended in 1842, "Thomas was kept strictly at church on Sundays as usual, till he knew the Morning and Evening Services by heart" (*Life,* pp. 9, 18). The atmosphere of his young life also seems to have been deeply influenced by a general increase in religious feeling throughout England, especially among the middle classes. The Oxford Movement had reached the Dorset clergy during the years in which he was growing up, and Evangelicalism had spread across the country during the decade before his birth in 1840.

But religious orthodoxy was only a cornerstone to the
fullness of the community in which Hardy spent his early
life. He and his father, a builder and a member of that
declining group in English society at the time, the yeoman
class, frequently led a band of musicians at jigs and fairs
throughout the region. At home, young Hardy used to
sit by the staircase each evening at sunset and recite hymns
to himself. His own description of the manner in which he
performed the daily ritual is perhaps most telling: "with
great fervency, though perhaps not for any religious reason,
but from the sense that the scene suited the lines." He called
himself, even in 1917, "churchy; not in an intellectual sense,
but in so far as instincts and emotions ruled" (*Life*, pp. 15,
376). The impression is that his religious sense as a child
was an expression of his general sensitivity, especially as it
found nourishment in the strength of the Dorset community. "In the actual course of Hardy's experience, his
'churchiness' and his attachment to the Dorset countryside
were inseparable, woven together into a single piety." [1] He
captures this essential aspect of his childhood in a poem
written years later, "Afternoon Service at Mellstock" (included in *Moments of Vision*):

> On afternoons of drowsy calm
> We stood in the panelled pew,
> Singing one-voiced a Tate-and-Brady psalm
> To the tune of "Cambridge New."

> We watched the elms, we watched the rooks,
> The clouds upon the breeze,
> Between the whiles of glancing at our books,
> And swaying like the trees.

> So mindless were those outpourings!—
> Though I am not aware
> That I have gained by subtle thought on things
> Since we stood psalming there.

1. Irving Howe, *Thomas Hardy*, p. 5. Howe's background sketch of
the early life, though brief, is perhaps the most balanced and fully
conceived of any by Hardy's biographers and critics.

The tension with which the poem concludes is a characteristic one for Hardy, emphasizing the ambivalence increasingly displayed in his fiction. His prose eventually casts this conflict as maddening, while, as here, his poetry is able to contain the contraries in the form of a lament for each of the battling alternatives.

At sixteen, Hardy became a pupil of John Hicks, an architect and church-restorer in Dorchester and a business acquaintance of his father. Hardy was "a born bookworm, that and that alone was unchanging in him; he had sometimes, too, wished to enter the Church; but he cheerfully agreed to go to Mr. Hicks's" (*Life*, p. 27). He had already begun to study French and the classics and was familiar by now with the Bible, the first book he knew thoroughly.[2] He continued his reading, though, while studying architecture, and entered into religious discussions with his fellow student Bastow, who began to impress on him the idea of adult baptism. The ardor with which Hardy plunged into research on the question, however, seems to have initiated some early doubts. Although "he was appalled at the feebleness of the arguments for infant christening, he incontinently determined to 'stick to his own side', as he considered the Church to be, at some costs of conscience" (*Life*, p. 29). In order to countenance his fellow pupil's arguments against the church in which he had been brought up, Hardy stopped reading "the heathen authors" to allow himself more time to study the New Testament. He began to apply his mind to questions of Christianity in general, apparently to strengthen his belief in church principles.

> Though he was younger than his companions he seems to have possessed a breadth of mind which they lacked; and while perceiving that there was not a shred of evidence for infant baptism in the New Testament, he saw that Christianity did not hang on temporary details that expediency might modify, and that the practice of

2. William Rutland, *Thomas Hardy: A Study of His Writings and Their Background*, p. 1.

an isolated few in the early ages could not be binding
on its multitudes in differing circumstances, when it
had grown to be the religion of continents. [*Life,*
p. 30]

Hardy's questionings at this point in his youth, however,
were only a prelude to the shocks he came to experience a
little later in his stay with Hicks.

Hardy came into direct contact with contemporary
thought through his friendship with Horace Moule, whom
he met in Dorchester. Moule, a Fellow of Queen's College,
Cambridge, whose father was vicar of the neighboring
Fordington, was just beginning his career as a writer for
the *Saturday Review* when he and Hardy became close.
Moule introduced him to the *Essays and Reviews* (1860),
a volume for a time even more controversial than Darwin's.
The authors' method probably impressed Hardy more than
their conclusions: their scientific approach to theology was
altogether new to him.[3] Moule must also have been responsible for introducing him to John Stuart Mill, whose *On
Liberty* appeared in 1859,[4] and, no doubt, to Darwin.
These readings most clearly reflect the rationalism to which
Hardy soon succumbed—indeed, embraced with enthusiasm
—during his stay in London beginning in April 1862. The
serene unity of the Dorset community became irreparably
damaged in his eyes as a result, although it was not until
nearly ten years later that signs of the disruption found
their way into his fiction.

3. Ibid., p. 53.
4. In a letter to *The Times* on the one hundredth anniversary of
Mill's birth (May 20, 1906), Hardy wrote that "we students [of the
1860s] knew almost by heart" the essay *On Liberty* (*Life,* p. 330). One
of Hardy's biographers glibly assumes Mill's influence by referring
to Sue Bridehead's quote from *On Liberty* in *Jude the Obscure*
(Rutland, p. 66). The author claims, incredibly enough, that *Jude*
"occupies a place by itself among Hardy's writings in that it was
primarily written for the sake of propagating certain ideas." But
there is in fact a heavy irony in Sue's reference to Mill; Hardy was
forlornly aware, by 1895, of the deceptive pathways of such philosophy.

Hardy's reading of Darwin—either in Dorchester, through his association with Moule, or soon afterwards in London—no doubt helped to confirm his growing rationalism. But the importance of his exposure to *The Origin of Species* lies only partly in Darwin's conscious effect on his mental development. The concrete result of Hardy's reading Darwin during this period of his life can be suggested by an early poem such as "Hap" (1866), where the poet, like Darwin's critics and biographers generally, neglects one of the deepest turns in *The Origin*. The significance of the artist's experience with *The Origin* in the wake of his first confrontation with rationalism is, rather, a symbolic one that establishes a parallel between Darwin's work and the development of Hardy's fiction—a parallel that throws the development of the novels into a relief that reveals its historical contours. The first movement in the novels involves simply the infection of the rural community by an urban rationalism, the conflict between Hardy's "churchiness" and his conversion to the rational creed. But with *The Return of the Native,* a new pattern is established, one that pits the necessarily revolutionary Darwin against the already stale midcentury rationalism of the early novels.

During the voyage of the *Beagle,* Darwin still sought the key to evolution in the exterior environment, in climate and natural surroundings. Even back in England, examining his specimens, his search for the evolutionary mechanism had led him to seek for the causes of change in the environment rather than in an organism's interior structure. He finally arrived at the clue he needed when he became aware that species respond actively to their environment. "The key change in the intellectual climate of the nineteenth century came with the recognition of adaptation, of the fact that creatures fit themselves to their environment." [5] But the concern with an exterior struggle and external determinism following the publication of *The Origin* for decades diverted even biologists from an important aspect of Darwin's insight—the dynamics of the

5. Loren Eiseley, *Darwin's Century,* p. 196.

living organism's interior system. Thus, even though Darwin himself broke the tension that accompanied "New Enlightenment" rationalism—whether circumstances or internal factors were determinant—the response, not only of the favorable public, but of biologists as well as so-called philosophers and social thinkers, indicates a common predisposition not to turn to the nature of the changing organism itself for an understanding of ongoing, lawful processes. The point is important because, as we shall see, it provides one explanation for the appearance of two voices in Hardy's late work: the first, the heir of the rationalism of an age that tended to attribute determinism more to the external than to the interior or individual world; the other, in conflict with, or bypassing, this perspective, and dwelling on the internal movement of the organism (or the individual) itself.

It is not so much whether Hardy, consciously or unknowingly, assimilated the subtle turn in Darwin's achievement that concerns us. What is significant is that both men performed similar feats of insight which, though unrecognized in the minds of their contemporary readers, seem to define a crucial shift in the intellectual climate of the time when viewed from a historical perspective.

During the voyage of the *Beagle* (1831–36), Darwin was impressed by the differences in structure of plants and animals on neighboring islands in the Galapagos:

> the most remarkable feature in the natural history of this archipelago . . . is that the different islands to a considerable extent are inhabited by a different set of beings. . . . I never dreamed that islands about fifty or sixty miles apart, and most of them in sight of each other, formed of precisely the same rocks, placed under a quite similar climate, rising to a nearly equal height, would have been differently tenanted.[6]

Darwin sought with difficulty to explain these phenomena. "It was evident that such facts as these," he writes in his

6. Charles Darwin, *Journal of Researches (The Voyage of H.M.S. Beagle)*, p. 359; observations made in September–October, 1835.

Autobiography, "as well as many others, could be explained on the supposition that species gradually become modified; and the subject haunted me." [7] But while he believed that such occurrences must be viewed within an evolutionary framework, he did not yet possess the key to its mechanism. Thus, in the journal of the *Beagle,* he hesitatingly offers the only explanation conceivable at the time, the effect of external conditions:

The only light which I can throw on this remarkable difference in the inhabitants of the different islands is that very strong currents of the sea, running in a westerly and W.N.W. direction, must separate, as far as transportal by the sea is concerned, the southern islands from the northern ones; and between these northern islands a strong N.W. current was observed, which must effectually separate James and Albemarle islands.

He suggests the effects of the current only after dismissing other factors in the external conditions of the region:

As the archipelago is free to a most remarkable extent from gales of wind, neither the birds, insects, nor lighter seeds would be blown from island to island. And, lastly, the profound depth of the ocean between the islands, and their apparently recent (in a geological sense) volcanic origin, render it highly unlikely that they were ever united; and this, probably, is a far more important consideration than any other, with respect to the geographical distribution of their inhabitants. Reviewing the facts here given, one is astonished at the amount of creative force, if such an expression may be used, displayed on these small, barren, and rocky islands; and still more so at its diverse yet analogous action on points so near each other. I have said that the Galapagos archipelago might be called a satellite attached to America, but it should rather be called a group of satellites, physically similar, organically distinct, yet intimately related to each other, and all

7. Charles Darwin, *Autobiography (1809–1882),* pp. 118–19.

related in a marked, though much lesser degree, to the great American continent.[8]

His remarks about this period of his work in the *Autobiography*, however, illustrate the status of these early investigations in relation to his later insights:

> But it was equally evident that neither the action of the surrounding conditions, nor the will of the organisms (especially in the case of plants), could account for the innumerable cases in which organisms of every kind are beautifully adapted to their habits of life. . . . I had always been much struck by such adaptations, and until these could be explained it seemed to me almost useless to endeavour to prove by indirect evidence that species have been modified.[9]

In June 1842, Darwin wrote "a very brief abstract" of his theory, which he had developed after reading Malthus in October 1838.[10] While the 1842 abstract is far from the succinct elaboration of the theory in the 1859 *Origin*, key changes have, of course, already occurred. In the third paragraph we find Darwin grappling precisely with the question of external conditions, but the context of the discussion is now the activity of organisms against the backdrop of environment (Darwin begins here, as in *The Origin*, with "Variation Under Domestication"):

> The nature of the external conditions tends to effect some definite change in all or greater part of offspring. . . . But more important is that simple generation,

8. Darwin, *Journal of Researches*, p. 363.

9. Darwin, *Autobiography*, p. 119.

10. Ibid., p. 120. Francis Darwin, the author's son, and editor of the 1842 abstract (along with the longer and more detailed 1844 sketch of what became *The Origin of Species*), notes in his introduction that the 1842 manuscript "was hidden in a cupboard under the stairs which was not used for papers of any value, but rather as an overflow for matter which [his father] did not wish to destroy" (Charles Darwin, *The Foundations of the Origin of Species: Two Essays Written in 1842 and 1844*, p. xvii).

especially under new conditions when no crossing,
causes infinite variation and not direct effect of external conditions. [*Foundations*, p. 2]

Darwin, though, is quick to place the human observer in
perspective, especially since he deals initially with domesti-
cated breeding:

man judges solely by his eye, and knows not whether
nerves, muscles, arteries are developed in proportion
to the change of external form. [*Foundations*, pp.
9–10]

The movement of the author's perspective has become
clearer. It is almost as if he were cautioning our reading as
well as suggesting the changes and difficulties in his own
observations. The subsequent tone of *The Origin* is also
suggested:

Introduce here contrast with Lamarck,—absurdity of
habit, or chance or external conditions making a woodpecker adapted to a tree.[11]

His concern is increasingly with the "structure of each
organism." He also issues another warning: "Be it remem-
bered that no naturalist pretends to give test from external
characters of species" (*Foundations*, pp. 42, 49).

By the time Darwin wrote *The Origin of Species* he was
in a position to resolve the exemplary problem noted
during the voyage of the *Beagle*. In looking beyond the
effects of external conditions for the mechanism of evolution, Darwin was finally able to recognize the creative
nature of "the struggle for existence"[12] and its formative
role in the origin and evolution of species. "Bearing in
mind that the mutual relations of organism to organism are

11. Darwin, *Foundations*, p. 10. The image of the woodpecker is a
favorite of Darwin's when he seeks to diminish the importance of the
effects of conditions; we shall, of course, see it again.

12. The famous phrase was originally Charles Lyell's in 1830.
Charles Lyell, *Principles of Geology*, 2 (1834): 391; quoted in Eiseley,
pp. 101–02.

of the highest importance, we can see why two areas having nearly the same physical conditions should often be inhabited by very different forms of life." [13] The structure of an organism, then, is primarily determined by its response to other organisms and to the environment rather than by the direct effect of external conditions. "From these considerations," concludes Darwin, "I think we need not greatly marvel at the endemic and representative species, which inhabit the several islands of the Galapagos Archipelago, not having universally spread from island to island" (*Origin*, p. 389).

In his preliminary "Historical Sketch" of the scientific literature on the subject of the origin of species, Darwin notes with particular emphasis the 1844 *Vestiges of Creation*, the work of a scientific amateur, Robert Chambers, who published his book anonymously at the time. Since the publication of Lyell's *Principles of Geology* (1830), all the ideas necessary for an evolutionary theory were existent; it only needed someone to fit the pieces together. While *The Vestiges* drew the first controversial attention to the idea of evolution, the book did not convince the professionals because it was the work of an amateur. Some of Darwin's remarks on Chambers's work clearly indicate this aspect of the situation:

> The work, from its powerful and brilliant style, though displaying in the earlier editions little accurate knowledge and a great want of scientific caution, immediately had a very wide circulation. In my opinion, it has done excellent service in this country in calling attention to the subject, in removing prejudice, and in thus preparing the ground for the reception of analogous views. [*Origin*, p. 58]

But Darwin is more concerned with, among other theoretical shortcomings, Chambers's contention that an impulse exists in nature " 'to modify organic structures in ac-

13. Charles Darwin, *The Origin of Species*, p. 394. "The edition published here is the first edition" (p. 49).

cordance with external circumstances' " (*Origin*, p. 57). He responds with the use of the image that, as we have noted, is a favorite of his when dealing with the problem of external conditions: "I cannot see that we thus gain any insight how, for instance, a woodpecker becomes adapted to its peculiar habits of life" (*Origin*, p.58).

In his introduction, Darwin suggests the context in which his work must be seen when he indicates that it is "of the highest importance to gain a clear insight into the means of modification" and "the coadaptations of organic beings to each other and to their physical conditions of life" (*Origin*, p. 67):

> In considering the Origin of Species, it is quite conceivable that a naturalist, reflecting on the mutual affinities of organic beings, on their embryological relations, their geographical distribution, geological succession, and other such facts, might come to the conclusion that each species had not been independently created, but had descended, like varieties, from other species. Nevertheless, such a conclusion, even if well founded, would be unsatisfactory, until it could be shown how the innumerable species inhabiting this world have been modified, so as to acquire that perfection of structure and coadaptation which most justly excites our admiration. Naturalists continually refer to external conditions, such as climate, food, etc., as the only possible cause of variation. In one very limited sense, as we shall hereafter see, this may be true; but it is preposterous to attribute to mere external conditions, the structure, for instance, of the woodpecker, with its feet, tail, beak, and tongue, so admirably adapted to catch insects under the bark of trees. In the case of the misseltoe, which draws its nourishment from certain trees, which has seeds that must be transported by certain birds, and which has flowers with separate sexes absolutely requiring the agency of certain insects to bring pollen from one

flower to the other, it is equally preposterous to account for the structure of this parasite, with its relations to several distinct organic beings, by the effects
of external conditions, or of habit, or of the volition
of the plant itself. [*Origin*, pp. 66–67]

It is, of course, the mechanism of evolution that is the
subject of Darwin's investigation, "understanding how
species arise in nature" (p. 114). By his third chapter,
"Struggle for Existence," he is ready to place the role of
conditions within the dynamic perspective of his theory:

The action of climate seems at first sight to be quite
independent of the struggle for existence; but in so far
as climate chiefly acts in reducing food, it brings on
the most severe struggle between the individuals,
whether of the same or of distinct species, which subsist
on the same kind of food. [*Origin*, p. 114]

It is always tempting, however, to isolate external conditions as if they were the major determinant:

When we travel from south to north, or from a damp
region to a dry, we invariably see some species getting
rarer and rarer, and finally disappearing; and the
change of climate being conspicuous, we are tempted
to attribute the whole effect to its direct action. But
this is a very false view. [*Origin*, p. 121]

It is also interesting to note a passage in the chapter that
speaks against the view of some writers on Hardy that the
artist, through his reading of Darwin, was made aware of
the tyranny of chance and accident in a hostile, or at
least an indifferent, world of nature. Yet what the young
Hardy would actually have read is:

When we look at the plants and bushes clothing an
entangled bank, we are tempted to attribute their
proportional numbers and kinds to what we call
chance. But how false a view is this! [*Origin*, p. 125]

Similarly:

> I have hitherto sometimes spoken as if the variations
> . . . had been due to chance. This, of course, is a
> wholly incorrect expression, but it serves to acknowl-
> edge plainly our ignorance of the cause of each particu-
> lar variation. [*Origin,* p. 173]

We can see, however, how the term could "acknowledge"
Hardy the rationalist's virulent perplexity in the face of
the "entangled bank" of life.

Stanley Edgar Hyman sees the image of the tangled
bank as central to the organizing vision of *The Origin*—
indeed, as the core of "essentially a modern vision." [14]
The inventiveness of Darwin's argument lies precisely in
his view of a single organism's "infinitely complex relations to other organic beings and to external nature"
(*Origin,* p. 115)—like the developing Hardy, the vision of
life becomes more and more one that man cannot grasp,
much less judge, "solely by his eye." The struggle for life
that occurs against the background of external nature becomes concretized in detail within the individual organism,
while the details themselves suggest the infinitude of
dynamic relations that are always present: "the structure of
every organic being is related, in the most essential yet
often hidden manner, to that of all other organic beings,
with which it comes into competition for food or residence,
or from which it has to escape, or on which it preys"
(*Origin,* p. 127).

Thus, Darwin's argument moves to a higher level in the
next chapter on "Natural Selection" where, now that a
perspective has been established, he elaborates the workings
of the evolutionary mechanism:

> We may conclude, from what we have seen of the in-
> timate and complex manner in which the inhabitants
> of each country are bound together, that any change

14. Stanley Edgar Hyman, *The Tangled Bank: Darwin, Marx,
Frazer, and Freud as Imaginative Writers,* pp. 32–33.

> in the numerical proportions of some of the inhabi-
> tants, independently of the change of climate itself,
> would most seriously affect many of the others.

> Nor do I believe that any great physical change, as of
> climate, or any unusual degree of isolation to check im-
> migration, is actually necessary to produce new and un-
> occupied places for natural selection to fill up by
> modifying and improving some of its varying inhabi-
> tants. [*Origin*, pp. 131, 132]

It seems fitting, then, that Darwin is moved to comment
on the limitation of human perspectives in relation to
the fullness of nature. The tone is surer, even darker, than
that of 1842, and provides still another aid to viewing the
development of Hardy's novels:

> Man can act only on external and visible characters:
> nature cares nothing for appearances, except in so far
> as they may be useful to any being. She can act on
> every internal organ, on every shade of constitutional
> difference, on the whole machinery of life. [*Origin*,
> p. 132]

Again, Darwin reminds us of the portrait-like emblem in
which the whole of nature is epitomized—"the structure
of the adult," "the structure of each individual" (p. 135).
In Whitehead's words, "[t]he organism is a unit of emergent
value." [15]

In the beginning of his fifth chapter, "Laws of Variation,"
Darwin deals finally and directly with the status of the
effects of external conditions in relation to the evolutionary
mechanism:

> How much direct effect difference of climate, food,
> etc., produces on any being is extremely doubtful. . . .
> We may, at least, safely conclude that such influences
> cannot have produced the many striking and complex
> co-adaptations of structure between one organic being

15. Alfred North Whitehead, *Science and the Modern World*, p. 10.

and another, which we see everywhere throughout nature.

When a variation is of the slightest use to a being, we
cannot tell how much of it to attribute to the accumu-
lative action of natural selection, and how much to
the conditions of life. Thus, it is well known to furriers
that animals of the same species have thicker and better
fur the more severe the climate is under which they
lived; but who can tell how much of this difference
may be due to the warmest-clad individuals having
been favoured and preserved during many generations,
and how much to the direct action of the severe climate? for it would appear that climate has some direct
action on the hair of our domestic quadrupeds.
Instances could be given of the same variety being
produced under conditions of life as different as can
well be conceived; and, on the other hand, of different
varieties being produced from the same species under
the same conditions. Such facts show how indirectly the
conditions of life must act. Again, innumerable instances are known to every naturalist of species keeping
true, or not varying at all, although living under the
most opposite climates. Such considerations as these
incline me to lay very little weight on the direct action
of the conditions of life. Indirectly, as already re-
marked, they seem to play an important part in affect-
ing the reproductive system, and in thus inducing
variability; and natural selection will then accumulate
all profitable variations, however slight, until they
become plainly developed and appreciable by us.
[*Origin,* pp. 174–75]

In the closing pages of *The Origin,* Darwin briefly alludes
to a concern that seems to hover silently over the entire
book: "Psychology will be based on a new foundation,
that of the necessary acquirement of each mental power
and capacity by gradation. Light will be thrown on the

origin of man and his history" (*Origin,* p. 458). The development of the human mind is an even newer evolutionary concern than the origin of species. And just as Darwin
argued that we must see with more than the eye, that we
must look beyond the realm of externals if we are to know
the full rhythms of life, he opened an analogous, and even
more foreboding, kingdom to view as his investigation,
for the moment, concluded.

One of Hardy's biographers sums up the intellectual
atmosphere of Darwinism, the world the artist entered as
he became a man, in terms of two dominant ideas: "firstly,
that the Primal Cause was Immanent in the Universe, not
transcendent to it; and, secondly, that the individual
human being was of very small significance in the scheme of
things. All the critics are agreed that these two conceptions
are those which dominate all Hardy's work." [16] And yet I
would suggest that these readers of Hardy have not read
deeply enough. As we have seen, to interpret Darwin's
influence in terms of two such ideas, ignoring completely
the revolutionary discovery of the self-regulating adaptation
of life to the environment, is to miss much of Darwin's
unique achievement. Of course, it can be argued that
Hardy, like others of his time, saw only the aspect of
external struggle in Darwin. But it would seem that it is
precisely the same static reading of Darwin that grants these
critics only a superficial reading of Hardy himself. The
tension in Darwin's own work—his search for the mechanism of evolution and the resulting key change in the intellectual climate when he realized that an interior system
within the organism responds actively to the environment—

16. Rutland, p. 56. Examples of shortsighted readings of Hardy are
numerous, mostly along the lines of Georg Roppen's remark in a
chapter on Hardy in *Evolution and Poetic Belief* (Webster, of course,
is another of Hardy's biographers quoted in the present study): Hardy's
intellectual development "is, as Webster has so well shown, a drama
whose climax might be said to come at the beginning when Hardy
was just twenty years of age." He goes on to quote from "Hap" (pp.
287–88).

provides a parallel to the tension in Hardy's own work. I would transform those two ideas that "dominate" Hardy into: first, an immanence in terms of an ongoing, dialectical process (where any mention of or search for a Primal Cause arises as a rational reaction to the ongoing drama, as an attempt to understand or explain it); second, even though the individual is of small significance against the backdrop of nature, his response to the environment (his interior life) becomes more and more important to us as a result of our awareness that his reactions are a key to the movement of life itself.

We cannot be sure whether Hardy read these important books before he went to London or early during his residence there. At any rate, the impact of the new ideas and his move to the capital form a single episode in his life. When he actually moved to London in April 1862, the "pink-faced youth" (in his own words, *Life,* p. 36) was undoubtedly amazed at the speed and pressure of life as it contrasted with provincial Dorchester. Young men of great ambition seemed to characterize the professional world he encountered in the city. "The major worry was 'failure.' . . . So great was the physical and mental strain that many men, it was said, were forced 'to break off (or to break down) in mid-career, shattered, paralysed, reduced to premature inaction or senility.' " [17] On the afternoon of his arrival, the young architect fresh from the country was greeted in the following manner by an acquaintance's cousin, when he inquired for a room: " 'Wait till you have walked the streets a few weeks . . . and your elbows begin to shine, and the hems of your trousers get frayed, as if nibbled by rats! Only practical men are wanted here' " (*Life,* p. 35). His first real contact with urban life must have disturbed him at least as much as the new ideas and methods he was discovering through his reading and conversation.

Hardy soon became an assistant architect with Arthur

17. Walter E. Houghton, *The Victorian Frame of Mind, 1830–1870,* p. 61.

Blomfield's firm. Blomfield's other pupils were "Tory and Churchy young men" (*Life,* p. 37), and Hardy was exposed to contemporary political conflicts firsthand when his fellow students engaged in satirizing the firm's upstairs neighbors, members of the Reform League, an advanced democratic group that once solicited Swinburne to sit in Parliament. He spent a few evenings a week at the Exhibition that began in London in 1862, and read a great deal. He began to show a preoccupation with a possible career in letters; even in Dorchester his reading had testified to this preoccupation. His constant effort to keep up with the literature of the period in spite of his job and the distractions of London reveals his serious intentions. His note about his study of Newman indicates his still increasing rationalism:

> A great desire to be convinced by him because Moule likes him so much. Style charming, and his logic really human, being based not on syllogisms but on converging probabilities. Only—and here comes the fatal catastrophe—there is no first link to his excellent chain of reasoning and down you come headlong. [*Life,* p. 48]

He was also reading the *Saturday Review* regularly, in which Moule was appearing. The periodicals continued their concern with evolution; the *Saturday Review* for 1864, for example, contained three articles directly addressed to the question.[18]

At the age of twenty-five, Hardy was still considering entering the Church, but his changed feelings about religion finally led him to abandon the idea: "[it] fell through less because of its difficulty than from a conscientious feeling, after some theological study, that he could hardly take the step with honour while holding the views which on examination he found himself to hold" (*Life,* p. 50). He was growing more and more interested in poetry, and be-

18. Harvey Curtis Webster, *On A Darkling Plain: the Art and Thought of Thomas Hardy,* p. 30.

came immersed in writing and studying verse during his
tenure at Blomfield's.

Two notes recorded during these days in London indirectly show the nature of his poetic concerns at a time
when he formed "the quixotic opinion that . . . in verse
was concentrated the essence of all imaginative and emotional literature" (*Life*, p. 48):

> May (1865) ". . . In architecture, men who are clever
> in details are bunglers in generalities. So it is in every-
> thing whatsoever."

> June 19 (1866). "A widely appreciative mind mostly
> fails to achieve a great work from pure far-sightedness.
> The very clearness with which he discerns remote pos-
> sibilities is, from its nature, scarcely ever co-existent
> with the microscopic vision demanded for tracing the
> narrow path that leads to them." [*Life*, pp. 48, 55]

The two thoughts form a paradox: the ability to weave
detail is necessary for the construction of a great work, yet
the capacity to envision such a work is apparently irrecon-
cilable with the means needed to achieve it. While Hardy
was thinking specifically of poetry at this time, the relation
of these ideas to his entire literary production is, of course,
incontrovertible. It is as though the sensibility that creates
the process underlying the vision, and thus sustains it, is in
conflict with the mind that forms the idea itself. Hardy's
sympathy seems to lie with the "widely appreciative mind"
that can perceive the general—a suggestion as to why he
preferred poetry to fiction. For, what is a novel if not a
series of microscopic visions, the particulars of experience
traced in detail? That this dramatic sensibility is, by implication, inferior in Hardy's mind to the generalizing vision
associated with the poet, seems quite plausible, given our
knowledge that he considered prose inferior to verse. In
other notes during this same period, he wrote:

"A certain man: He creeps away to a meeting with—
his own sensations."

"He feels himself shrink into nothing when contem-
plating other people's *means* of working. When he
looks upon their *ends,* he expands with triumph."

"There is no more painful lesson to be learnt by a
man of capacious mind than that of excluding general
knowledge for particular." [*Life,* p. 55]

Again, echoes of the same paradox; and while the place-
ment of Hardy's sympathies is not as strong as it was above,
a similar conflict is expressed. The "widely appreciative
mind" ("a man of capacious mind") here finds the pain of
weaving details precisely in his need to exclude the general; and although the phrasing is ambiguous, our interpretation might read that he may triumphantly regard the
exterior of other people ("their *ends*"—the general) while
he is reduced to nothing when he attempts to contemplate
the interior ("their *means*"—the particular). As we shall see
in our reading of the novels, the presence of a tension based
in such issues is central to the fictional world Hardy was to
create.

In 1867, Hardy left London, on leave from Blomfield's,
and returned to work at Hicks's in Dorchester. He went back
to the country because of the city's ill effect on his health,
but his retreat also seemed the result of mental depression.[19]
His dissatisfaction with architecture, his social isolation,

19. Lois Deacon and Terry Coleman's *Providence and Mr. Hardy*
has made a rich speculative addition to Hardy studies. The authors
attempt to establish the artist's secret five-year engagement to his
cousin, Tryphena Sparks, beginning in 1867, and then to assert that
she was in fact his niece. Much of their case is documented through
the use of Hardy's work, both the prose and the poetry. The suggestion is that the Tryphena motif is of central importance to his
writings and that her image in many ways guides his work. The theory
is tenuous as historical fact; the authors' methods seem questionable
indeed. Yet, as an imaginative hypothesis, the idea is chillingly
attractive. It is also compatible with the reading of Hardy attempted
in my study. Still, what finally did direct Hardy's imagination,
though strongly suggested here as well as in the Tryphena hypothesis, must, I think, remain an open question.

and his quandary as to the choice of a course in life must have intensified the disillusionment effected by his loss of faith in God and in man's formerly exalted place in nature. Having always been seriously preoccupied with literature, it was in that direction that he looked for the future:

> Almost suddenly he became more practical, and queried of himself definitely how to achieve some tangible result from his desultory yet strenuous labours at literature during the previous four years. He considered that he knew fairly well both West-country life in its less explored recesses and the life of an isolated student cast upon the billows of London with no protection but his brains. [*Life,* p. 56]

He realized that the only way to succeed in a practical way with literature was to write prose fiction. He turned to the novel with a frank realization that he meant to use literature as a means to worldly success, leaving for awhile the purer realms of poetry. The manner in which he began his first novel indicates the practical nature of that pursuit in his eyes: "So down he sat in one of the intervals of his attendances at Mr. Hicks's drawing-office (which were not regular), and, abandoning verse as a waste of labour— though he had resumed it awhile on arriving in the country —he began the novel," *The Poor Man and the Lady,* the manuscript of which is lost to us now (*Life,* pp. 56–57; Hardy also studied Wilkie Collins's technique in order to arrive at a commercially successful style). The materials on which Hardy drew for the novel—his knowledge of "both West-country life in its less explored recesses and the life of an isolated student cast upon the billows of London"— are a paradigm, even at this first exploratory plunge into fiction, for the two sensibilities whose dialectic is to initiate the development of his novels. Two other aspects of Hardy's description of the lost book in the *Life* are also clear forerunners of tensions we shall find in examining the fiction— first, that the subject of the story is the result of the conclusions of a formerly religious young man who has recently come under the spell of rationalist techniques and inquiry:

> a striking socialistic novel—not that he mentally de-
> fined it as such, for the word had probably never, or
> scarcely ever, been heard of at that date. . . . The
> story was, in fact, a sweeping dramatic satire of the
> squirearchy and nobility, London society, the vul-
> garity of the middle class, modern Christianity, church-
> restoration, and political and domestic morals in
> general, the author's views, in fact, being obviously
> those of a young man with a passion for reforming the
> world—those of many a young man before and after
> him; the tendency of the writing being socialistic, not
> to say revolutionary. [*Life,* pp. 56, 61]

and second, that his stylistic aim was to write clearly to the point of transparency: "the writing being socialistic, not to say revolutionary; yet not argumentatively so, the style having the affected simplicity of Defoe's [which had long attracted Hardy]" (*Life,* p. 61). The potential conflict be-tween the sources and the methods involved in this early work, as well as between the elements within each cate-gory alone, will become clearer after an examination of his full production in prose.

Hardy's description of himself as "churchy; not in an intellectual sense, but in so far as instincts and emotions ruled," signifies his inheritance of a rural, or community, sensibility, expressed here in his knowledge of "West-country life in its less explored recesses." But the intel-lectual sense, too, dominated him at least as much as the emotional. It was his assimilation of the rationalism of contemporary thought that destroyed his early orthodoxy; and that, as a result, necessarily came into conflict with the residual layer of "churchy" emotion and instinct, the sinews of the community from which he sprung. The rational mode of thought he adopted after his initial confrontation with the new influences symbolized the response of the "isolated student cast upon the billows of London with no protection but his brains." For one who participated in the rural sense of community, such protection was unnecessary; but given the infecting influence of rational thought, the bonds of community became weakened. This progression is most clearly recorded in Hardy's early novels, from *Under the Greenwood Tree* through *The Return of the Native*.[20] The fictional world centers around the community rather than the individual in this first phase, as the abiding power of emotional or social ties is systematically weakened by rational invasion in the form of urban intrusions into Wessex.

At the same time, however, the result of such tension could only be the same reductio that rationalism in general was to experience: by stripping away all illusions by the power of individual reason, the individual becomes isolated and renders himself the object of study. The next natural step, then, is to turn those incisive analytic powers upon the self: at this juncture, Hardy's fiction took a frightful, yet even more powerful, turn. This movement came together for the first time with *The Mayor of Casterbridge*, the moment of departure for his last, and probably best, novels. But at this point the dialectic of conflicting sensibilities becomes so intense that, not only does the truth of the isolated ego take over the content of the story; the means of its recognition are simultaneously driven past the discoveries themselves, as the style seems to overcompensate by lapsing into philosophical editorializing or pseudo-scientific language. At times, the fictional world only barely holds itself back from outright conceptualization.

Ironically, Hardy's dramatic sense, apparently buried under the rubble of the dying community, had to restrain his rational sense in order to sustain the reality of the new world. By the time he wrote his last novel, *Jude the Obscure*, the degree of tension was unbearable and he was forced, more by his own demands than by the response of

20. This study begins examination of the novels with *Under the Greenwood Tree* rather than with *Desperate Remedies;* my emphasis is the Wessex world.

the public, to abandon fiction and return to poetry. By bringing each sensibility to bear upon the other in his description of his very first novel, *The Poor Man and the Lady*—an urban or rational sensibility (the isolated individual) and a rural or emotional sensibility (the community) —Hardy showed, even in 1867–68, full possession of all the elements his novels were to contain. He needed only to place them in dynamic relationship for the inexorable dialectic to begin.

By the time Hardy entered his thirties, the rationalism that had affected him so strongly in his twentieth year had virtually gained the day. Leslie Stephen was one of the most outspoken and influential rationalists of the time, and Hardy records the effects of his friendship many times in the autobiography. They met in 1873 when, as editor of the *Cornhill* magazine, Stephen asked for the serial rights to *Far From the Madding Crowd*. Once Hardy became intimate with him, he wrote that it was Stephen "whose philosophy was to influence his own for many years, indeed, more than that of any other contemporary" (*Life,* p. 100). The same tense admixture of an uncompromising intellectual rationalism with a high degree of emotional sensitivity that characterized Hardy was also true of Stephen. Hardy recorded on July 1, 1879 a remark by his friend, whose criticism influenced him as deeply as did his philosophy:

> "The ultimate aim of the poet should be to touch our hearts by showing his own, and not to exhibit his learning, or his fine taste, or his skill in mimicking the notes of his predecessors." [*Life,* p. 128]

Stephen's mental development, like his temperament, paralleled Hardy's to an astonishing degree. His family life had also been deeply religious; Stephen's parents were among the foremost circle of Evangelical homes in the country at the height of the religious revival. His loss of faith and conversion to rationalism were similar to Hardy's, both temporally and in the influences that shattered belief. Stephen's biographer assigns the final cause of his loss of

faith to the appearance of Darwin's *Origin*.[21] With the overthrow of the foundations of belief in his reading of Darwin, he began a study of German philosophy and the
Higher Critics, including Hegel, Strauss, and Renan, as
well as of Comte. The combination of Mill's *Logic* with the
straightforward style of an Evangelical heritage were the
basis of the initial hopes of Stephen's generation. "Truth
exists in a palpable form for Victorian rationalists. . . .
[They] had found a method to discover truth.[22] But Stephen
disliked the crudity of rational reformers, and by 1874
found unbearable the optimism of his friend Henry Faw-
cett, the man who first introduced him to the rational creed
at Cambridge. Utilitarianism, like Evangelicalism, was also
subject to doubt, since both saw their own version of
verifiable experience as being final. It was Hardy whom
Stephen asked to witness his renunciation of Holy Orders
in March 1875:

> The deed was executed with due formality. Our con-
> versation then turned upon theologies decayed and
> defunct, the origin of things, the constitution of matter,
> the unreality of time and kindred subjects. [Stephen]
> told me that he had "wasted" much time on systems
> of religion and metaphysics, and that the new theory of
> vortex rings had a "staggering fascination" for him.[23]

Stephen's influence on Hardy's thinking must, at first,
have intensified the rationalism he had already developed
on his own. Yet Hardy's belief in reason could never be
complete, whether his intellect would have it or not. One
of Stephen's most determined roles was that of the moralist;

21. Noel Annan, *Leslie Stephen*, p. 162. Annan's chapter on Stephen's
loss of faith provides a summary of A. O. Lovejoy's argument, in
The Great Chain of Being, that the theory of evolution transformed
the entire structure of orthodox metaphysics since Plato and called
into question, not only belief, but the traditional order of thought
itself (chap. 5).

22. Annan, pp. 144, 148.

23. Frederic W. Maitland, *The Life and Letters of Leslie Stephen*,
p. 264 (Hardy's description, quoted in *Life*, pp. 105–06).

as a literary critic, even more than as a historian, he looked at writers in terms of their ethics and their philosophies. Hardy, who once said he would have been happy as a university don, must have been susceptible to Stephen's predispositions; for the philosophical tone, the knowledge of generalities, permeates his poetry and creates tension in his fiction. We come right to the point in Stephen's essay on Wordsworth:

> In practice the utterance of emotions can hardy be dissociated from the assertion of principles. The imagination reasons. The bare faculty of sight involves thought and feeling. The symbol which the fancy spontaneously constructs, implies a whole world of truth or error, of superstitious beliefs or sound philosophy. The poetry holds a number of intellectual dogmas in solution; and it is precisely due to these general dogmas, which are true and important for us as well as the poet, that his power over our sympathies is due. If his philosophy has no power in it, his emotions lose their holds upon our minds, or interest us only as antiquarians and lovers of the picturesque. But in the briefest poems of a true thinker we read the essence of the life-long reflections of a passionate and intellectual nature. . . . The rational and the emotional nature have such intricate relations that one cannot exist in great richness and force without justifying an inference as to the other.[24]

As we inferred earlier, Hardy believed "that poetry epitomized the knowlede of generalities he coveted." [25] It was in writing his novels, however, that Hardy was forced to occupy himself with details, the interior life of individuals ("their *means*"), and the dynamic process of human relationships. It was well after he had given up fiction that he explicitly stated the precarious stance we shall see ex-

24. Leslie Stephen, *Hours in a Library*, vol. 2, "Wordsworth's Ethics," pp. 272–73.
25. Webster, pp. 52–53.

hibited there: "Rationalists err as far in one direction as
Revelationists or Mystics in the other; as far in the direction
of logicality as their opponents away from it" (*Life,* p. 332).

In Stephen, too, signs of the limits of rationalism began
to show, whether he saw them himself or not. Given the
emotional as well as the intellectual similarities between
Hardy and Stephen, an awareness of the latter's limits
points implicitly to those places where the artist was still
free to go. Stephen "unwittingly got imprisoned by his own
categories." [26] And yet the men of Stephen's and Hardy's
generation were aware of the bankruptcy of their perspective; in Hardy's note on his friend in 1901 lies a comment
on the entire thrust of his own fiction:

> May 11. Leslie Stephen says: "The old ideals have
> become obsolete, and the new are not yet constructed.
> . . . We cannot write living poetry on the ancient
> model. The gods and heroes are too dead, and we
> cannot seriously sympathize with . . . the idealized
> prize-fighter." [*Life,* p. 308]

We shall see more evidence for this perspective in the
increasing tension between the conceptual and dramatic
tendencies in the development of Hardy's novels.

But while the artist was at least able to explore dramat-
ically insights which his intellect could neither express nor
deal with, the rationalist of the same generation could go
no deeper than the limits of his conceptual understanding.
The latent implications of the parallel achievements of
Darwin and Hardy might be seen in both the conceptual
and the imaginative aspects of the generation following the
period of Hardy's career as a novelist. The strain that
racked the world of ideas in a perspective like Stephen's
was relieved when Darwin's metaphorical suggestions toward a real psychology blossomed with the advent of
psychoanalysis, a conceptual rendering of the heavy labor
of Hardy's late novels. Similarly, a D. H. Lawrence, a
Proust, a Joyce worked alongside the new conceptualists.

26. Annan, p. 241.

Even by the 1880s, a flood of optimism was sustained by the majority of intellectuals, especially the social philosophers. Material prosperity caused businessmen and economic thinkers to continue to believe that what men wanted from life could be attained through a continuation of processes ongoing in society. Their basic hope and expectation lay in their faith in the future development of natural science and its analogue, the science of society, as well as in the energy of the individual. The optimistic philosophy that Hardy had read earlier—especially Herbert Spencer and Comte—retained its widespread influence. But the real basis of these hopeful systems was becoming clear to a few like Hardy. A rational thinker like Stephen could see limitations in such systems, but only from a point of view that questioned results rather than method. Stephen perceived something amiss because the reasoning itself was not completely truthful or rigorous, not because he doubted the assumptions from which truth could be reached. As a thinker, Hardy, too, seemed to retain some kind of faith in the intellect; we have seen how he was influenced so deeply by Stephen's rationalism. He perceived at this time not that the social order was in accord with natural processes; his intellectual interpretation of Darwin ran just the other way: that nature was hostile to man.

But, again, Hardy was able to express his darkening view in ways beyond the rational. While his biographers and most of his critics assign "the deepening and darkening of his inspiration" to "the canker of thought" alone,[27] we shall see that his intellectual, or conceptual, tendencies are not identical with the deepest impulses in his fictional universe. Even though it is true that "Hardy was appreciated for *Under the Greenwood Tree* and *Far From the Madding Crowd,* and [was] viewed primarily as a rural idyllist long after the tragic scope of his intention as a novelist had been revealed in *The Return of the Native*," [28] it is the tension

27. Rutland, p. 89.
28. Helen Lynd, *England in the Eighteen-Eighties,* p. 63.

within what has been called his "pessimism" that concerns us, not simply the fact of his darkening vision. "Having reached a stage of spiritual vacuum by about 1880, Hardy seems to have set about trying to fill it by reading philosophy." [29] Even in his own conscious life, Hardy appears to have retained that very faith in the mind's ability to discover truth that he progressively undermines in the development of his novels.

The shortsightedness of one of his biographers, which may reflect the artist's own unconsciousness of the nature of his creations, provides an excellent example of where we shall find the strongest indications of conflicting impulses in Hardy's fiction. Having noted that Schopenhauer (whom Hardy was reading in translation during the late 1880s) devotes the fourth book of *The World as Will and Idea* to "the denial of the will to live," Rutland quotes from the doctor's pronouncement about Little Father Time's suicide in *Jude the Obscure*: "He says it is the beginning of the coming universal wish not to live." [30] His point is that the novel is an expression of Hardy's adoption of the philosophical views he encountered in his reading. But the biographical interpretation contains two flaws. First, Hardy goes on to say that the child "was their [Sue and Jude's] nodal point, their focus, their expression in a single term" (*Jude,* p. 406); the pronouncement on Father Time is an embodiment of the relationship between the lovers. The doctor's statement (no doubt taken from Schopenhauer) is Hardy's lapse into a poetic generalization (the contemplation of other people's *"ends,"* when the visionary "expands with triumph"), an impulse which rises up against the drama of the couple's actual relationship ("people's *means* of working"). We shall see that Hardy shifts within the novel from a narrative voice that attempts to be "refined out of existence" ("the microscopic vision demanded") —the voice that, at first, suggests a journey into Jude's consciousness alone, but that subsequently introduces Sue

29. Rutland, p. 89.
30. Ibid., p. 99.

Bridehead to sustain the dramatic process because it cannot invent interior monologue—to an omniscient and editorializing narrative voice that rebels against silence and needs to state "general knowledge" on top of dramatic "particular." Second, Rutland's reading assumes in the first place that *Jude* was written primarily to expound certain ideas; that the fact that it is a novel is secondary to the "fact" that is was written as an exposition of a "philosophy." [31] While Hardy did use Schopenhauer in the doctor's statement, the place of that remark in the fictional world is an expression of conflicting narrative voices *within the novel,* not a sign that the life of Hardy's intellect is identical to the life of his imaginative creations.

That Hardy labored under conflicting tendencies has been recognized:

> What he would like to believe—and sometimes did— was constantly at war with what his intellect told him to be the truth. He could not escape the painful consciousness of the "cursed condition of humanity." Born under one law, he felt himself bound by another.[32]

But the nature of the conflict, its successive stages, and the abiding tension that unifies Hardy's imagination is revealed only in a close reading of the novels. The conflict between his intellect and his desires only initiates the pattern of his fiction; once set in motion, the outcome of the dialectic is almost inevitable.

31. Rutland claims, for example, that *Tess* and *Jude* "are, in essence, literature of another category from that to which Hardy's novels belong. They are didactic; not incidentally or occasionally, but deliberately and consistently" (p. 221).

32. Webster, p. 88.

2 The Early Novels

Under the Greenwood Tree
A Pair of Blue Eyes
Far From the Madding Crowd

Hardy's life as an architect's pupil in Dorchester when he was twenty was "a triple existence unusual for a young man —what he used to call, in looking back, a life twisted of three strands—the professional life, the scholar's life, and the rustic life, combined in the twenty-four hours of one day, as it was with him through these years" (*Life,* p. 32). He describes his peculiar situation at the time as the result of the "accident" that he worked in a country town which was just beginning to feel the effects of modern life ("railways and telegraphs and daily London papers"); "yet not living there, but walking in every day from a world of shepherds and ploughmen in a hamlet three miles off, where modern improvements were still regarded as wonders, he saw rustic and borough doings in a juxtaposition peculiarly close" (*Life,* pp. 31–32).

Hardy's life at this time was an almost literal version of the multiple sensibilities displayed in his early fiction. While the architecture student set about the tasks of church restoration and the like during the working day, the young poet read Greek tragedy in his spare time and reluctantly gave up the study only on the advice of his friend Moule, who urged him to find a means of income in the profession chosen for him. In fact, speculation in the *Life* suggests that, had Hardy been advised to continue his studies of Greek plays and give up architecture, he might have gone on to the university instead of to London where he sought to further his professional career. Though Hardy's fiction is hardly autobiographical, the flavor of his life as a young man in Dorchester, the admixture of life styles, and the tension between his real situation and his desires read like the novels he was to write.

The early novels—*Under the Greenwood Tree, A Pair of Blue Eyes,* and *Far From the Madding Crowd*—span the period from Hardy's last professional connection with architecture in London to his establishment as a successful popular author. Together they represent the initial world of his imagination, with *Far From the Madding Crowd,* the first of the Wessex novels, symbolizing the crystallization of an independent and complete imaginative universe. The original impulses of the creator of Michael Henchard and Jude Fawley deserve special consideration because the world of these early books forms the fundamental structure of Hardy's entire production in prose. This initial mythology establishes a seminal world in which Jude's fate seems the inevitable outcome of the original pattern. It is as though Hardy's early work defines the distinctively individual aspects of his creations, while the later novels reflect the finally explicit and full-blown statement of the same mind after the experiences of twenty-five years that saw the decline of the Victorian climate.

Hardy the novelist was, above all, a teller of tales. Even after finishing *Far From the Madding Crowd,* he wrote to Leslie Stephen, his editor at the time:

> The truth is that I am willing, and indeed anxious, to give up any points which may be desirable in a story when read as a whole, for the sake of others which shall please those who read it in numbers. Perhaps I may have higher aims some day, and be a great stickler for the proper artistic balance of the completed work, but for the present, circumstances lead me to wish merely to be considered a good hand at a serial. [*Life,* p. 100]

Some notes on the writing of fiction recorded in July 1881 indicate the area of his concern in prose:

> The writer's problem is, how to strike the balance between the uncommon and the ordinary so as on the

one hand to give interest, on the other to give reaility.

In working out this problem, human nature must never be made abnormal, which is introducing incredibility. The uncommonness must be in the events, not in the characters; and the writer's art lies in shaping that uncommonness while disguising its unlikelihood, if it be unlikely. [*Life*, p. 150]

Hardy's narrative style remained firmly traditional throughout his career as a novelist and points to the central importance of the story itself in all of his fiction. In the early novels, the nature of his imaginative world is clearly reflected in the way character and event are created.

The nature of the existing social and natural order in the idyllic world of *Under the Greenwood Tree* and *Far From The Madding Crowd* is one of thoroughgoing community. Hardy "accepts the assumptions of the society that he depicts, and neither apologizes for it nor condescends to it." [1] But, at the same time, this ordered world unknowingly harbors refugees from the future, doubting and disturbing forces that move secretly within the pastoral landscape until, at crucial moments, their alien character is betrayed. *A Pair of Blue Eyes,* a highly idiosyncratic departure from the Wessex of the other two early books,[2] sustains perhaps best of all Hardy's early work the deep and complex array of cross-purposes and disturbed dreams that exist within an apparently consistent world. What he was to write of Jude applies with not a little irony to Hardy himself at this initial period of his career, and to the unknown and complex nature of his early fictional world:

He would accept any employment which might be offered him on the strength of his late employer's recommendation; but he would accept it as a provisional thing only. This was his form of the modern vice of unrest.

1. Donald Davidson, "The Traditional Basis of Thomas Hardy's Fiction," in *Still Rebels, Still Yankees,* p. 58.

2. While *Under the Greenwood Tree* is not a Wessex novel proper, its flavor, as well as its geography, places it in that imaginative environment.

Moreover he perceived that at best only copying, patching and imitating went on here; which he fancied to be owing to some temporary and local cause. He did not at that time see that medievalism was as dead as a fern-leaf in a lump of coal; that other developments were shaping in the world around him, in which Gothic architecture and its associations had no place. The deadly animosity of contemporary logic and vision towards so much of what he held in reverence was not yet revealed to him.[3]

One feels that the young Hardy meant to believe in the the community he created in his first novels. It seems he did not recognize at first the implications of the quiet doubts that make *Under the Greenwood Tree* a deceptively perfect "rural painting"; that he resisted the secret and dark side of Henry Knight's nature; and that he thought he had succeeded in reestablishing happiness, or at least quietude, at the end of *Far From the Madding Crowd.*

The 1912 preface to *Under the Greenwood Tree* includes some curiously suggestive remarks about Hardy's view of his early work in later years:

In rereading the narrative after a long interval there occurs the inevitable reflection that the realities out of which [the tale of the Mellstock Quire] was spun were material for another kind of study of this little group of church musicians than is found in the chapters here penned so lightly, even so farcically and flippantly at times. But circumstances would have rendered any aim at a deeper, more essential, more transcendent handling unadvisable at the date of writing; and the exhibition of the Mellstock Quire in the following pages must remain the only extant one, except for the few glimpses of that perished band which I have given in verse elsewhere.

An earlier preface written in 1896 noted with "regret the displacement of these ecclesiastical bandsmen by an isolated

3. *Jude the Obscure,* pp. 68–69.

organist . . . and despite certain advantages . . . secured
by installing a single artist, the change has tended to
stultify the professed aims of the clergy, its direct result
being to curtail and extinguish the interest of parishioners
in church doings." The story of the replacement of the
Mellstock Quire by the new vicar's harmonium interweaves
with the tale of Dick Dewy and Fancy Day's romance. A
love affair set against the backdrop of a social event establishes very clearly a pattern fundamental to Hardy's fiction
and, in the case of *Under the Greenwood Tree,* furnishes a
gentle but explicit account of the way character and event
help to define each other in the imaginative environment.

The opening scenes depict a joyous communion of the
Mellstock community on Christmas eve, with the choir and
their rounds of caroling throughout the neighborhood as
the focal point. The evening's tour is a traditional event
in local history, but this Christmas marks a break with the
past because of the choir's knowledge that the new vicar
intends to replace them in church with a single organist.

> "Times have changed from the times they used to
> be," said Mail, regarding nobody can tell what interest-
> ing old panoramas with an inward eye, and letting his
> outward glance rest on the ground because it was as
> convenient a position as any. "People don't care much
> about us now! I've been thinking we must be almost
> the last left in the county of the old string players.
> Barrell-organs, and the things next door to 'em that
> you blow wi' your foot, have come in terribly of late
> years." [p. 24]

As early as the fourth chapter, the tension between an old,
ordered world and a new, externally imposed interference,
forms the social landscape of the novel. On reaching the
schoolhouse, where Fancy Day, the new teacher and future
organist has just settled in, the choir forms a portrait of
the fading past:

> Then passed forth into the quiet night an ancient and
> timeworn hymn, embodying a quaint Christianity in

words orally transmitted from father to son through
several generations down to the present characters,
who sang them out right earnestly:

> Remember Adam's fall,
> O thou Man;
> Remember Adam's fall
> From Heaven to Hell.

[pp. 26–27]

While the hymn is addressed to the new teacher, there is,
strangely, no response from the schoolhouse; after two
more encores, there is still no answer. Just as the group,
disturbed by the silence, is ready to depart, a light shines
from the window and Fancy makes her first appearance.
The symbolic confrontation between two worlds is strongly
suggested, with faint whispers of both the Eustacia and the
Sue Bridehead of the future:

> a young girl framed as a picture by the window archi-
> trave, and unconsciously illuminating her countenance
> to a vivid brightness by a candle she held in her left
> hand, close to her face, her right hand being extended
> to the side of the window. She was wrapped in a white
> robe of some kind, whilst down her shoulders fell a
> twining profusion of marvellously rich hair, in a wild
> disorder which proclaimed it to be only during the
> invisible hours of the night that such a condition was
> discoverable. Her bright eyes were looking into the grey
> world outside with an uncertain expression, oscillating
> between courage and shyness, which, as she recognized
> the semi-circular group of dark forms gathered before
> her, transformed itself into pleasant resolution. [p. 29]

The passage is loaded with an almost unconscious knowledge of the power lurking behind these early scenes. The
threatening "wild disorder" of the deep night revealed to
the embodiment of the old order is the kind of uncommonness in events that Hardy considered so central to the
art of fiction. Indeed, against the commonplace landscape

of the winter night and the choir, the chapter introduces a series of such events, which tie together the characters who will eventually enact the drama of the book.

The carolers' next stop is Farmer Shiner's house.[4] It is Shiner who will court Fancy against the wishes of Dick Dewy, the choir-member who, at this point, mysteriously disappears.

But it is not until after the party stops at the church for refreshment that his absence is noticed. The brief scene in the church, too, reaches symbolic significance for the developing story:

> In the pauses of conversation there could be heard through the floor overhead a little world of undertones and creaks from the halting clockwork, which never spread further than the tower they were born in, and raised in the more meditative minds a fancy that here lay the direct pathway of Time. [p. 32]

Dick is soon found swooning beneath Fancy's window where he has remained since the choir left the schoolhouse. His father, Tranter Dewy, drags him away as the choir proceeds to its next stop, the vicarage. Mellstock's new young vicar, Mr. Maybold, like the new schoolteacher, at first responds to the caroling with silence. But, after a moment, "a musical voice was heard exclaiming from inner depths of bedclothes—'Thanks, villagers!'" (p. 34). As the chapter concludes, the tranter, like his father William, Dick's grandfather, softly notes that something is a bit strange on this Christmas eve.

Hardy's description of Christmas morning in the church neatly crystallizes the progress of the story. Dick, seated with the choir, is struck by Fancy's arrival at the service: "A new atmosphere seemed suddenly to be puffed into the ancient edifice by her movement, which made Dick's body

---

4. Shiner's house "by day [had] the aspect of a human countenance turned askance, and wearing a sly and sicked leer"; but which, hidden at night, showed only "the outline of the roof upon the sky" (p. 30).

and soul tingle with novel sensations" (p. 39). It is not so much that Fancy herself represents a new world that threatens the established community; it is in her pivotal position in the story, a role which is not fulfilled until late in the novel, that she forms the link between *Under the Greenwood Tree*'s only hint of the external urban world, the new vicar Maybold (a force which becomes more and more explicit in the later novels, and which occurs in very muted form only here), and the Wessex environment in the person of Dick Dewy. Hardy's conception of woman is at the center of what later becomes an obvious tension between worlds but which, in these early works, has not yet recognized itself. Fancy, then, is attractive not only to Dick. Maybold feels "the same instinctive perception of an interesting presence, in the shape of the same bright maiden" (p. 40). Thus, the implications of the love story become symbolic of broader social forces only suggested in *Under the Greenwood Tree*, but which become part of a pattern that emerges more clearly even as early as the next two novels. In fact, the story seems to point toward the underlying tensions no matter which perspective is invoked. "The poetry of a scene varies with the minds of the perceivers. Indeed, it does not lie in the scene at all" (*Life*, p. 50). While this note in Hardy's diary seems to contradict his conception of the importance of the event, it reveals instead the richness of his notions of plot. For Dick, it is Fancy's presence in the church that creates a "new atmosphere." But this "new atmosphere" is perceived by Dick only on a personal level, while its implications are greater than he can possibly imagine now or ever know in the future.

While Hardy was no stylistic or technical innovator in the sense that he exploited perspectives or cognitive processes for new approaches to the novel, his sense of story included the recognition of an array of perceptions within his imaginative world. That world lives only when events become important to the characters. An individual's change of fortune affects not only himself but the community as well, whether the character be a member of the community or an outsider—thus, "the writer's art lies in shaping the

uncommonness of events while disguising its unlikelihood,"
and the poetry of a given scene lies in the reality of those
events for the characters. In order to sustain his fictional
world, the artist creates an entire social order in which uncommon events may occur with credibility and in which
his characters may breathe. But the nature of the events
Hardy creates within his world involves the disturbance of
the order sustaining those occurrences: here lies the tension
within the imaginative environment, a tension he did not
at first recognize. This inevitable conflict in the dialectic
of character and event is the result of the kinds of characters
with which Hardy peopled his world. Those figures who
are part of the natural community in his novels—natives
of Wessex for the most part—are essentially fixed or non-
developing.

> The changeless characters of the Wessex world are of
> both minor and major order; and they are generally
> set in juxaposition with one or two characters of a
> more changeful or modern type. The interplay between
> the two kind of characters is the focus of the struggle
> that makes the story. Hardy is almost the only modern
> novelist who makes serious use of this conflict and at
> the same time preserves full and equal respect for both
> sets of characters. . . .
>
> Nature, itself unchangeable and inscrutable, is the
> norm, the basis of Wessex life. . . .
>
> Nearest to nature, and therefore most changeless,
> are the rustics . . . who throng Hardy's pages. In the
> rural comedies, like *Under the Greenwood Tree* and
> *Far From the Madding Crowd,* they dominate the
> scene. Only the vicar, in *Under the Greenwood Tree,*
> with his newfangled church organ, and perhaps in a
> slight way Sergeant Troy in the other novel, foreshadow
> the kind of disturbance set up by the changeful
> character.[5]

5. Davidson, pp. 58–59. Hardy's critics, with few exceptions, seem
to align themselves either with the view that he worked in isolation
from the climate of the day, or that he was a perfect representative
of it. Davidson's apparent misunderstanding of the nature of the

Davidson's view is extremely useful in defining the nature
of the population of Hardy's world; but he is, unfortu-
nately, too cautious in his reading of the early novels. He
insists that Hardy wrote in terms of the assumptions of his
Wessex world and, thus, against the pattern of his age.
But in attempting to unify his theory of the traditional
basis of Hardy's fiction, he refuses to entertain the development of the novels seriously and would have difficulty in
understanding the more explicit attitudes and conflicts of
A Pair of Blue Eyes, as well as of the later Hardy. It seems
that the very nature of Hardy's fiction was rooted in an
unconsciously perceived set of tensions that find their expression in conceptions like the dissolution of an ordered
community in the face of modern disturbance, but which,
in the early Wessex works, only gently reveal themselves.
A Pair of Blue Eyes, as we shall soon see, is the exception
among the early novels, and practically defines itself as
such in its unique, even puzzling, urbanity.

The story lines in *Under the Greenwood Tree* cross con-
tinually, at times to the point of identity. The suspicion
that Shiner is at the bottom of the choir's displacement
arises when some of the villagers realize it is the courting
farmer who is trying to install Fancy as the organist in
order to further his own amorous designs. From one point
of view, then, the entire plot may be read as one of the
rustics says: " 'Then the music is second to the woman, the
other church-warden is second to Shiner, the pa'son is
second to the church-wardens, and God A'mighty is nowhere at all' " (p. 92).

The capricious woman and her romantic relationships
to the central male figures is the most definitive character
aspect of the universe of Hardy's novels. Fancy Day represents in embryo the procession of women to appear as
central figures in plot and conception in the future. And

world of the early novels stems from his overlooking Hardy's final
view of nature in the two books following *Under the Greenwood
Tree*, a view which casts serious doubts on a nonillusory, natural
basis for the ordered Wessex community.

while Hardy's women may seem more acted upon than acting, their inability to accept responsibility for their attractiveness, much less their actions, is crucial to the effect they
have upon their lovers and upon the society in which they
live. Even Fancy is the prototype of Sue Bridehead, "oscil-
lating between courage and shyness" because of an unrest
that Hardy seems to believe inherent in modern women.[6]
Although Fancy herself does not represent the outside intruder in the pastoral world, her response to the young
vicar, despite her engagement to Dick Dewy, sets upon her
the responsibility of maintaining the integrity of an ordered
world before the temptation of an outsider. Maybold is
the only character in *Under the Greenwood Tree* who may
be construed as an interference from the external world;
indeed, he is the only figure in the book who is able to
control himself in spite of what he feels, and thus who is
capable of change within the story.

Yet the question of Fancy's responsibility is enough to
align her with disturbing forces in the social landscape
while, at the same time, she is inextricably bound to the
community through Dick. Although Maybold is the outsider, his responses to the events of the story often coincide
most clearly with the overview of the artist. As we shall
soon see, the outsider seems to be the only character granted
a broad perspective resembling that of the author himself.
Even though Maybold loved her during her first perform-
ance at the organ "as he had never loved a woman before"
(p. 177), he immediately retracts his offer of marriage on
learning of her former engagement to Dick. He recognizes,
in spite of the shock, "that the young creature whose graces
had intoxicated him into making the most imprudent
resolution of his life was less an angel than a woman"
(p. 187).

6. The question of Hardy's conception of the nature of woman is
an important but extremely difficult one, especially because of the
pivotal importance of female figures in his novels. Whether he believed
women to be inherently irresponsible and restive, or only symbolic
of a characteristic sensitivity either social or historical, remains an
open question.

As the outsider, it is Maybold who disturbs Fancy and Dick even after they are able to overcome the prejudices of her father. And even though the vicar is responsible enough to retract, the damage to the community has been done through Fancy's original acceptance of his offer. In a sense, Hardy has rewritten the myth of the Fall by representing the potential of sin in the outsider, the response to temptation by woman, and her contamination of the existing community by her own fall. The irony of the hymn sung by the choir outside Fancy's window on Christmas eve ("Remember Adam's fall,/O thou Man") is brought home by the end of the novel. Even though Maybold urges Fancy to tell Dick of their brief liaison, she decides to keep it "a secret she would never tell" (p. 211).

It is in Hardy's conception of woman that the tension between the old order and "modern unrest" becomes real in the world of his novels. Fancy, in her receptiveness to the tempter (himself inherently innocent but dangerous within the web of circumstance), has become an agent of disturbing forces. But, at the same time, she is bound to the community through her engagement to Dick. For all practical purposes, the novel ends happily. But *Under the Greenwood Tree* is deceptively unified: the doubt left by Fancy's secret causes the novel to remain, in a sense, open-ended; the community is now susceptible to infection from the outside. The breach of contract and trust, while healed in deed, remains an open wound in moral terms, a violation of the integrity of the old order.

Although *A Pair of Blue Eyes* was written directly after *Under the Greenwood Tree,* it is best to consider *Far From the Madding Crowd* at this point because it shares the Wessex that has virtually been established in the tale of the Mellstock Quire. *A Pair of Blue Eyes,* as we have noted, departs from the landscape of Wessex itself and, while thematically it deals with matters almost identical to the other two early works, its curious emphasis is enough to earn it special consideration.

The preface to *Far From the Madding Crowd* notes "a

break of continuity in local history" that occurs in Wessex
(or in the corresponding model in the real world—one cannot be sure) shortly after the period of the narrative. The
change issues from the supplanting of the class of station-
ary cottagers in the region by migratory workers, an event
which symbolically announces the separation of the native
inhabitants from the soil, a rupture in "the indispensable
conditions of existence" that were the basis of an entire
history and tradition.

Weatherbury embodies the agrarian community. The
sheep-shearing scene in Bathsheba's barn defines the traditional world in all its unified aspects. The barn "not
only emulated the form of the neighborhood church of
the parish, but vied with it in antiquity" (p. 164); in
fact,

One could say about this barn, what could hardly be
said of either the church or the castle, akin to it in
age and style, that the purpose which had dictated its
original erection was the same with that to which it
was still applied. Unlike and superior to either of
those two typical remnants of medievalism, the old
barn embodied practices which had suffered no mutilation at the hands of time. Here at least the spirit of the
ancient builders was at one with the spirit of the
modern beholders. Standing before this abraded pile,
the eye regarded its present usage, the mind dwelt upon
its past history, with a satisfied sense of functional
continuity throughout—a feeling almost of gratitude,
and quite of pride, at the permanence of the idea which
had heaped it up. The fact that four centuries had
neither proved it to be founded on a mistake, inspired
any hatred of its purpose, nor given rise to any reaction that had battered it down, invested this simple
grey effort of old minds with a repose, if not a grandeur, which a too curious reflection was apt to disturb
in its ecclesiastical and military compeers. For once
medievalism and modernism had a common standpoint.

The lanceolate windows, the time-eaten arch-stones and chamfers, the orientation of the axis, the misty chestnut work of the rafters, referred to no exploded fortifying or worn-out religious creed. The defence and salvation of the body by daily bread is still a study, a religion, and a desire. . . .

This picture of to-day in its frame of four hundred years ago did not produce that marked contrast between ancient and modern which is implied by the contrast of date. In comparison with cities, Weatherbury was immutable. The citizen's *Then* is the rustic's *Now*. In London, twenty or thirty years ago are old times; in Paris ten years, or five; in Weatherbury three or four score years were included in the mere present, and nothing less than a century set a mark on its face or tone. Five decades hardly modified the cut of a gaiter, the embroidery of a smock-frock, by the breadth of a hair. Ten generations failed to alter the turn of a single phrase. In these Wessex nooks the busy outsider's ancient times are only old; his old times are still new; his present is futurity.

So the barn was natural to the shearers, and the shearers were in harmony with the barn. [pp. 164–166]

The central characters in the novel perform within and against this Wessex landscape. Gabriel Oak, of course, is the quintessential representative of the community. As he tends his flock in the opening scenes of the book, the harmony between man and nature excudes peace: "The sky was clear—remarkably clear—and the twinkling of all the stars seemed to be but throbs of one body, timed by a common pulse" (p. 9). And while the order of nature is in harmony with man, humanity still retains its uniqueness against the backdrop of the heavens in the form of Oak's flute: "Suddenly an unexpected series of sounds began to be heard in this place up against the sky. They had a clearness which was to be found nowhere in the wind, and a sequence which was to be found nowhere in nature. They were the notes of Farmer Oak's flute" (p. 10). But, in spite of the harmony, the pronouncement might be taken as foreboding. "In making even horizontal and clear inspections we colour and mould according to the wants within us whatever our eyes bring in" (p. 16). The mute tension results from the quiet doubt whether nature is intrinsically ordered, or whether it is man who imposes an order on nature (and thus on himself as well)—an order that becomes an illusion of harmony when his wishes do not supplant his needs.

Even with Oak, the feeling that his inner peace, though sustained throughout the novel despite immense disappointments and troubles, is often precarious is occasioned by his initial responses to Bathsheba and our knowledge that he continues to love her throughout the book: "Having for some time known the want of a satisfactory form to fill an increasing void within him, his position moreover affording the wildest scope for his fancy, he painted her a beauty" (p. 16). The pattern established in *Under the Greenwood Tree*, the pivotal importance of woman, returns; Oak, like Dick Dewey, never recognizes the wound the community has received through his lover's fall. For Bathsheba, like Fancy Day, succumbs to the external tempter and remains morally infected, even with the apparent reestablishment of peace and order by marriage at the end of the novel.

The poetics of *Far From the Madding Crowd* follow those of the earlier work; the pattern, of course, continues as well. All the central characters except one are members of the community. Its laws rule that Oak must step aside for Boldwood to court Bathsheba and, as the most thoroughgoing symbol of Weatherbury, Gabriel resigns himself to his fortune not without good will. But the story really begins when the scene is invaded by Sergeant Troy. Ironically, Troy is a native of Weatherbury, while Bathsheba and Oak are not: but the woman-farmer and the shepherd belong to the community as Troy does not. Although Troy's presence alone is disturbing, he seriously influences the world of the novel through his attractiveness to Bathsheba. Again, it is the woman who forms the bridge between the two sensibilities.

Troy and Bathsheba meet for the first time very soon after the symbolic scene in the shearing barn, as if to emphasize the coming drama directly in terms of the plot. Their meeting also follows Boldwood's initial display of interest in Bathsheba. Indeed, the ironies work almost identically to those in *Under the Greenwood Tree*. Just as the choir sings the hymn "Remember Adam's fall,/O thou Man" at Fancy's window, Hardy half-jokingly prefaces Bathsheba and Boldwood's first real encounter with "Adam had awakened from his deep sleep, and behold! there was Eve" (p. 133). And, since the implications of the allusion to the Fall of Man are as serious here as in the earlier work, the use of the reference is similarly displaced in the sequence of action. Bathsheba meets Boldwood early in the same day when she will encounter Troy, just as Dick and the choir see Fancy early in the same evening when the vicar belatedly greets the carolers.[7] It is also noteworthy that Dick sees Fancy for the first time on the day of a communal event, Christmas eve, in the same way that Boldwood meets Bathsheba on a similarly symbolic instance in terms of the community, the marketplace on a Saturday.[8]

Just before the marketplace encounter, Hardy momentarily illuminates the nature of Bathsheba's behavior as it affects the world of the novel. He also provides a touch of irony in the last words of the paragraph as if to indicate the coming events of the evening and the displaced occurrence of the insight presented:

7. While Boldwood and Dick are not specifically equated here (Oak finally emerges as Dick's parallel), at this point in the story Oak has given way to the farmer, and thus for the moment passes along his role. In terms of the structure of the community and its violation, Boldwood and Oak are interchangeable.

8. Even here, the parallels are more meaningful than is apparent— the marketplace denotes the functional values of Wessex, which were deemed even more real than the religious values in the shearing scene.

Material causes and emotional effects are not to be arranged in regular equation. The result from capital employed in the production of any movement of a mental nature is sometimes as tremendous as the cause itself is absurdly minute. When women are in a freakish mood their usual intuition, either from care-lessness or inherent defect, seemingly fails to teach them this, and hence it was that Bathsheba was fated to be astonished today. [p. 133]

The artist hints at the revelation of Bathsheba's character that both she and the world of social relationships will experience later in the novel. At the same time, he reestab-lishes on an explicit basis the nature of his poetics, as character and event work out their seemingly inevitable dialectic. Indeed, his use of the word *fated* in this passage suggests that atmosphere of doom and inevitability which almost reaches the stature of a law in the later novels and works on a level close to determinism in this early work. The interrelation of Hardy's poetics and the nature of his fictional world occurs as early as *Far From the Madding Crowd*; but not until the later works does the relation be-come glaringly explicit.

Bathsheba, like Fancy Day, occupies a position of respon-sibility with Boldwood that she does not recognize until too late. Even before Troy's arrival in her life, her inability to control her responses portends the far-ranging conse-quences suggested as early as the meeting at the market-place. She is potentially a danger to individual suitors be-fore Troy's intrusion renders her a threat to the community as well. "He was altogether too much for her, and Bath-sheba seemed as one, who facing a reviving wind, finds it blow so strongly that it stops the breath" (p. 213). But the underlying nature of her character remains inscrutable, a characteristic, it seems, of Hardy's women in general.

Bathsheba loved Troy in the way that only self-reliant women love when they abandon their self-reliance. When a strong woman recklessly throws away her strength she is worse than a weak woman who has never had any strength to throw away. One source of her inadequacy is the novelty of the occasion. She has never had practice in making the best of such a condition. Weakness is doubly weak by being new. [p. 214]

In the turmoil of her anxiety for her lover she had agreed to marry him; but the perception that had accompanied her happiest hours on this account was rather that of self-sacrifice than of promotion and honor. [p. 315]

While Bathsheba's relationship with Boldwood caused her a grim dejection, her response to Troy is frenzied; marriage and the death of Fanny Robin reduce her to near madness.

Bathsheba's marriage to Troy parallels, if not initiates, a noticeable breakdown in the community. The shearing barn, originally a symbol of the integrity of the community, becomes the symbol of its degeneration once Troy is master of the farm. The harvest feast becomes a drunken spectacle by the end of the evening, while Oak, typically, remains the one true preserver of order. Oak thinks at first that only Bathsheba's corn is exposed to the breeding storm: "All the night he had the feeling that the neglect he was labouring to repair was abnormal and isolated—the only instance of the kind within the circuit of the county" (p. 294). But Boldwood, through his own neglect, has also left his produce exposed to the inclement weather. It is as though an infectious lassitude has spread across the entire region, almost directly accountable to Troy's interference. Yet even the suggested decay of the community becomes irrelevant against the background of nature itself, symbolized by the explosion of the storm; "love, life, everything human, seemed small and trifling in such close juxtaposition with an infuriated universe" (p. 287). That the

importance of an event or a perspective is a function of
the perceiver was a point with Hardy from the first. He
notes in his diary as early as the end of December 1865:
"To insects the twelvemonth has been an epoch, to leaves
a life, to tweeting birds a generation, to man a year"
(*Life*, p. 55).

Bathsheba wanders tearfully about the countryside after
she has spent the night before Fanny Robin's funeral in
the woods. The full effect of the events of the novel finds
its expression in her perception of the coexistence of contraries in nature. It is man's puzzled response to a scene
recognized in all its fullness for the first time:

> There was an opening towards the east, and the
> glow from the as yet unrisen sun attracted her eyes
> thither. From her feet, and between the beautiful
> yellowing ferns with their feathery arms, the ground
> sloped downwards to a hollow, in which was a species
> of swamp, dotted with fungi. A morning mist hung
> over it now—a fulsome yet magnificent silvery veil,
> full of light from the sun, yet semi-opaque—the hedge
> behind it being in some measure hidden by its hazy
> luminousness. Up the sides of this depression grew
> sheaves of the common rush, and here and there a pe-
> culiar species of flag, the blades of which glistened in
> the emerging sun, like scythes. But the general aspect
> of the swamp was malignant. From its moist and poi-
> sonous coat seemed to be exhaled the essences of evil
> things in the earth, and in the waters under the earth.
> The fungi grew in all manner of positions from rotting
> leaves and tree stumps, some exhibiting to her list-
> less gaze their clammy tops, others their oozing gills.
> Some were marked with great splotches, red as arter-
> ial blood, others were saffron yellow, and others tall
> and attenuated, with stems like macaroni. Some were
> leathery and of richest browns. The hollow seemed
> a nursery of pestilences small and great, in the imme-
> diate neighborhood of comfort and health, and Bath-

sheba arose with a tremor at the thought of having
passed the night on the brink of so dismal a place.
[pp. 347–48]

The notes of Oak's flute early in the novel were an indication that man, no matter what the appearances of the moment, himself imposes a believable order upon nature
when his community is intact and his social relationships
viable. Thus, the recognition that nature is an impersonal
entity, separate from man even when he is a member of an
ordered community, suggests the underlying possibilities
of doubt and the dissolution of order. The quality of man's
perception of nature and the state of his community are
inseparable. *Far From the Madding Crowd* moves from
Oak's idyllic sheepherding (where the potential for the
later view is implicit) and the shearing episode in the barn,
where man and nature are in harmony and the social order
intact; through the vision of the storm and indifferent,
even hostile, nature on the night of the drunken harvest
feast in the same barn; to Bathsheba's disgust and bottom-
less despair at the sight of the swamp. The violation of
Fanny's grave by the flow of rainwater through a gargoyle
on the roof of the church drives the change in the perception of nature even further—to the point of its absolute
antipathy to man. Even though it continues to serve its
purpose of draining water, man's functional intentions
for the gargoyle have now taken on destructive tendencies.
Hardy is explicit: "The persistent torrent from the gargoyle's jaws directed all its vengeance into the grave"
(p. 362).

The perception of a hostile nature also provides, for
the first time, an insight into the sensational Troy. While
his outlines have been strongly drawn throughout the book
and his effect on the Wessex community made clear, it is
not until the curtain is drawn back across the entire landscape of the novel that any insight into his character
is possible. Troy is granted the equivalent to Maybold's
ability to control his actions, a glimpse of self-knowledge.

He is, in spite of his present role, still a geographical native
to Weatherbury and, in a sense, must involuntarily recognize his effect on the world that bore him with a kind of
contrition. His own past has handled him roughly; the
story of his life, for all its excitement, is the denial of a
home.

Almost for the first time in his life Troy, as he stood
by this dismantled grave, wished himself another man.
It is seldom that a person with much animal spirit
does not feel that the fact of his life being his own is
the one qualification which singles it out as a more
hopeful life than that of others who may actually resemble him in every particular. Troy had felt, in his
transient way, hundreds of times, that he could not
envy other people their condition, because the possession of that condition would have necessitated a different personality, when he desired no other than his
own. He had not minded the peculiarities of his birth,
the vicissitudes of his life, the meteor-like uncertainty
of all that related to him, because these appertained
to the hero of his story, without whom there would
have been no story at all for him; and it seemed to be
only in the nature of things that matters would right
themselves at some proper date and wind up well.
This very morning the illusion completed its disappear-
ance, and, as it were, all of a sudden, Troy hated himself. The suddenness was probably more apparent than
real. A coral reef which just comes short of the ocean
surface is no more to the horizon than if it had never
been begun, and the mere finishing stroke is what
often appears to create an event which has long been
potentially an accomplished thing.
He stood and meditated—a miserable man. Whither
should he go? "He that is accursed, let him be accursed
still" (Revelation, xxii, 11), was the pitiless anathema
written in this spoliated effort of his newborn solicit-
ousness. A man who has spent his primal strength in

journeying in one direction has not much spirit left for reversing his course. Troy had, since yesterday, faintly reversed his; but the merest opposition had disheartened him. To turn about would have been hard enough under the greatest providential encouragement; but to find that Providence, far from helping him into a new course, or showing any wish that he might adopt one, actually jeered his first trembling and critical attempt in that kind, was more than nature could bear.

He slowly withdrew from the grave. He did not attempt to fill up the hole, replace the flowers, or do anything at all. He simply threw up his cards and forswore his game for that time and always. [pp. 364–65]

During the years of uncertainty about her husband's possible death, Bathsheba's life is the embodiment of the tension that now exists within the community. When Troy is finally killed by Boldwood, his disturbing influence is at least eradicated, through action in a manner parallel to Maybold's retraction of his marriage offer to Fancy. But, like the situation at the end of *Under the Greenwood Tree,* the wound has already been inflicted—the effect on the original order is a mental, or moral, one. In spite of Hardy's attempts to gloss over the irreparable rift, in the form of Boldwood's pardon and Bathsheba's marriage to Oak, events have wrought changes in the very fabric of life. Bathsheba and Oak's love is indeed "strong as death" (p. 457); no other simile could describe it properly. It is a real love, nurtured by experience of the hardest kind. It seems that Hardy tried to resist the deepest impulses of these early works by performing marriages at the end of both *Under the Greenwood Tree* and *Far From the Madding Crowd.* On the other hand, the figure of Henry Knight in *A Pair of Blue Eyes* is Hardy's clearest and fullest portrait of the nature of these disturbing impulses at this point in his career. *A Pair of Blue Eyes* departs from the other two early novels precisely because of its powerful representation and forceful concern with a character like Knight; even the differences in setting between the second novel and the other two works might be attributed to this central departure in conception. It was perhaps this urge that Hardy was resisting when he turned to the writing of his third novel, *Far From the Madding Crowd*.[9] *A Pair of Blue Eyes* contains a power obviously missing in both his preceding and following works, a driving impulse perhaps too shaking for him to deal with at this time. But the force unquestionably existed in Hardy's mind and work from the very first. It became an original feature of his world even in its muted whispers in *Under the Greewood Tree,* and presented itself more and more forcibly as his art developed. The manner of his displacing the energy of a Knight in *Far From the Madding Crowd* resembles the way in which his women rehearse the effect of the inescapable future intruder in their initial romances. With Knight comes the explicit recognition of a first stage of conflict: "What [Hardy] would like to believe—and sometimes did—was constantly at war with what his intellect told him to be the truth." Before the tension of concept and drama comes the meeting of reason and desire.

The scene of *A Pair of Blue Eyes* is "the outskirts of lower Wessex." While the setting is different from those of the other early works, its background tone is essentially the same, although the novel's emphasis has shifted almost completely onto the three main characters. Hardy notes in his 1895 preface the "craze" for church restoration at the time of writing; he also furnishes a customary remark about the nature of the story and his characters:

9. Perhaps the reason for his declaration of Wessex at the time of *Far From the Madding Crowd* was a formal attempt to return to the world of *Under the Greenwood Tree,* which Hardy still thought relatively immune from the invasion of a Knight. Of course, "he had not the slightest intention of writing for ever about sheepfarming" after the third novel (*Life,* p. 102); but the actual nature of his long-range plans at this time are unknown.

To restore the grey carcases of a medievalism whose spirit had fled seemed a lot less incongruous act than to set about renovating the adjoining crags [of the rugged seaside] themselves.

Hence it happened that an imaginary history of three human hearts, whose emotions were not without correspondence with these material circumstances, found in the ordinary incidents of such church-renovations a fitting frame for its presentation.

In a 1912 postscript to the earlier preface, he ambiguously remarks, in a way similar to his later reflection on the writing of *Under the Greenwood Tree:* "In its action [the book] exhibits the romantic stage of an idea which was further developed in a later book." Referring to *The Woodlanders,* Hardy reinforces the implication that his early work is a very definite indication of what was to come.

The landscape of the novel, briefly, is virtually the same as that of *Under the Greenwood Tree* and *Far From the Madding Crowd.* The trinity of central figures, too, is identical to the triangles of the other two novels. Elfride Swancourt is Fancy and Bathsheba, with little difference in the way her character affects the structure of the story. Stephen Smith, while at first glance an outsider invading Endelstow from London, is in fact a native ("Judging from his look, London was the last place in the world that one would have imagined to be the scene of his activities", p. 10), performing a role parallel to those of Dick Dewy and the combination of Oak and Boldwood. The romance of Stephen and Elfride, which takes up the first part of the book, is also familiar by now. And, as usual, the artist peppers the environment of these early scenes with asides that lend a recognizable flavor to Endelstow, for example,

Strange conjunctions of phenomena, particularly those of a trivial everyday kind, are so frequent in an ordinary life that we grow used to their unaccountableness, and forget the question whether the very long

odds against such juxtaposition is not almost a dis-
proof of it being a matter of chance at all. [p. 74]

The connections between the nature of the story and
Hardy's ideas on the art of the novel are as visible here
as they are in his other early work.

The way in which the outsider's effects on the central
female character were forshadowed in *Under the Greenwood Tree* and *Far From the Madding Crowd* by a displaced recognition of the coming fall is repeated here in the
identical form of a portentous occurrence with the first
lover. In fact, the meeting of rural and urban, traditional
and modern sensibilities takes on explicitly symbolic form
in Elfride and Stephen's journey to London in order to
be married. Elfride, in her prohibited affair with Stephen,
experiences for the first time "an inner and private world
apart from the visible one about her" (p. 115). The coming
full-blown conflict of sensibilities is already suggested in
this early tension; the scene at Paddington Station is a
forceful indication of the glare of urban penetration into
the world of Endelstow, which finally arrives with Knight's
appearance.[10] The scene also describes Stephen's difficulty
in dealing with an intrusion made real to him only for the
first time; like Dick, Oak, and Boldwood, he feels its effect
in the loss of his beloved.

> "Is this London?" she said.
> "Yes, darling," said Stephen in a tone of assurance
> he was far from feeling. To him, no less than to her,
> the reality so greatly differed from the prefiguring.
> She peered out as well as the window, beaded with
> drops, would allow her, and saw only the lamps, which
> had just been lit, blinking in the wet atmosphere,
> and rows of hideous zinc chimneypipes in dim relief

10. The image of the window in the railway carriage foreshadows
the scene in Knight's rooms in London, where his window facing the
city street symbolizes a changing perception of the world and the
nature of the new urban sensibility.

against the sky. She writhed uneasily, as when a thought is swelling in the mind which must cause much pain at its deliverance in words. Elfride had known no more about the stings of evil report than the native wild-fowl knew of the effects of Crusoe's first shot. Now she saw a little further, and a little further still. [p. 124]

. . . What yesterday had seemed so desirable, so promising, even trifling, had now acquired the complexion of a tragedy. [p. 131]

Hardy could hardly have been more specific at this moment in the novel. The "thought swelling in the mind" and the coming "pain at its deliverance in words" (an apt metaphor for the bookish Knight) describe the drama of the future intrusion so aptly compared to that of Robinson Crusoe on the denizens of the island. The feeling of inevitability is woven into the very fabric of the fictional world to an extent even more explicit than in either of the other works of this period. Stephen, too, is sketched in these early moments in a way that indicates his role later in the novel. While he fancies himself Knight's protégé, he is really his mentor's antithesis. He is able to act and succeed in the world of community in the book—a community which, recognized as dissolving, even nonexistent, from more sophisticated perspectives, extends further than usual in the early novels. It is the world of London as well as Endelstow, the business world of the Victorian empire and the social ladder of English society. Stephen is not a brooding, restive intellectual like Knight; he is limited by his nature not to question, the basis of his ability to act and to succeed within the community.

It was a time when mere seeing is meditation, and meditation peace [on the meadows of Endelstow]. Stephen was hardly philosopher enough to avail himself of Nature's offer. His constitution was made up of very simple particulars; was one which, rare in the

springtime of civilizations, seems to grow abundant
as a nation gets older, individuality fades and edu-
cation spreads; that is, his brain had extraordinary
receptive powers, and no great creativeness. Quickly
acquiring any kind of knowledge he saw around him,
and having a plastic adaptability more common in
woman that in man, he changed colour like a chame-
leon as the society he found himself in assumed a
higher and more artificial tone. He had not many
original ideas, and yet there was scarcely an idea to
which, under proper training, he could not have
added a respectable coordinate. [pp. 101–02]

Hardy's description of Stephen during his evening walk
through Endelstow points precisely to those characteristics
which distinguish him from Knight, signs which assume the
proportion of historical statement when the two men are
later placed side by side in the story. His patience in waiting to hear from Elfride after his return from India com-
pletes the portrait: "This act of patience was in keeping
with the nature of a man precisely of Stephen's constitution" (p. 269).

Knight first enters the story when Stephen visits him
at his rooms in London. Hardy uses the present tense to
describe the inn and its position within the city; the scene
moves from the larger perspective of street life to the
isolation and curious intimacy of Knight's chambers. It is
as though the picture of the city and the inn is an abiding
one, comparable to the description of a natural landscape
in Wessex. The building is located in the center of the
flow of the antagonistic streams of urban life: "Bede's Inn
has this peculiarity, that it faces, receives from, and dis-
charges into a bustling thoroughfare speaking only of
wealth and respectability, whilst its postern abuts on as
crowded and poverty-stricken a network of alleys as are to
be found anywhere in the metropolis" (p. 141). The contradictions of urban society itself are invoked as a prelude
to Knight's entrance. He is first seen through Stephen's

eyes, as though Hardy wishes to wait before revealing the fullness of his character.

Stephen pushed aside the curtain, and before him sat a man writing away as if his life depended upon it—which it did.

A man of thirty in a speckled coat with dark brown hair, curly beard, and crisp moustache: the latter running into the beard on each side of the mouth, and, as usual, hiding the real expression of that organ under a chronic aspect of impassivity. . . .

Knight's mouth and eyes came to view now. Both features were good, and had the peculiarity of appearing younger and fresher than the brow and face they belonged to, which were getting sicklied o'er by the unmistakable pale cast. The mouth had not quite relinquished rotundity of curve for the firm angularities of middle life; and the eyes, though keen, permeated rather than penetrated: what they had lost of their boy-time brightness by a dozen years of hard reading lending a quietness to their gaze which suited them well. [pp. 142–43]

Knight's frenzied writing within the privacy of his rooms clashes sharply with the scene outside, just as Stephen's clean-shaven, clear complexion is in contrast with his friend's features. And, as if to emphasize even more strongly the array of perspectives evoked by the scene, the description also touches upon a world within Knight's world, the aquarium in the window. Stephen takes his friend's writing as evidence of his intimate personal knowledge of the many facets of life, including that which now most interests the younger man, the romantic. But Knight's response to Stephen's belief begins to define the essayist's isolation, giving detailed substance to the symbolic descriptions above:

"But, my dear Stephen, it is only those who half know a thing that write about it. Those who know it thoroughly don't take the trouble. All I know about wo-

men, or men either, is a mass of generalities. I plod
along, and occasionally lift my eyes and skim the wel-
tering surface of mankind lying between me and the
horizon, as a crow might; no more." [p. 146]

Here, Knight stands out even more clearly against Stephen's
ability to act within an order that his perceptions allow
him to believe in; his view of writing implies a vision of
the artist as a man unable to participate fully in life because of the nature of his perception of the world. That
world, in its urban representation, appears apart from the
perceiver, viewed at a distance:

> "There!" said Knight, "where is there in England a
> spectacle to equal that? I sit there and watch them
> every night before I go home. Softly open the sash."
>
> Beneath them was an alley running up to the wall,
> and thence turning sideways, and passing under an
> arch, so that Knight's back window was immediately
> over the angle, and commanded a view of the alley
> lengthwise. Crowds—mostly of women—were surging,
> bustling, and pacing up and down. Gaslights glared
> from butchers' stalls, illuminating the lumps of flesh
> to splotches of orange and vermilion, like the wild
> colouring of Turner's later pictures, whilst the purl
> and babble of tongues of every pitch and mood was
> to this human wild-wood what the ripple of a brook
> is to the natural forest. [pp. 148–49]

The antithesis represented by Knight and Stephen is
symbolized in the two articles Elfride holds as gifts from
each of her lovers, a check from Stephen's earnings in India
and Knight's present of earrings. "She almost feared to let
the two articles lie in juxtaposition: so antagonistic were
the interests they represented that a miraculous repulsion
of one by the other was almost to be expected" (p. 224)—
again, the foreboding of a nearly fateful pattern. The gifts
themselves represent the divergent natures of each suitor:
Stephen's proudly earned, yet impersonal gift of money,
the symbol of his community; and Knight's carefully chosen

and tender offering. In the same way that Troy told Bathsheba she was beautiful, a pronouncement Boldwood never knew to make, Knight's gift clarifies Elfride's final choice.

The scene of Knight's ordeal on the Cliff without a Name is perhaps the most powerful, and certainly the most sensational, in the novel. It also represents the point at which Elfride chooses him over her younger suitor. Stephen, coincidentally, is returning from India at precisely the same moment on a steamboat within view of the pair on the crags. Knight's vision as he hangs above the sea waiting for death is the central perspective in the book—it is the broadest, most comprehensive view of life attempted in any of the early works. It parallels Troy's fleeting vision of himself in the graveyard and Bathsheba's in the woods but far surpasses both. Knight, of course, is the only figure in *A Pair of Blue Eyes* who could be granted the experience. It is a black vision of the universe and of man's place in the cosmos, seen with the certainty offered only by death, free from any attempt to order the blinding chaos of human experience. Knight keenly approximates the consciousness of the artist as the veil is lifted from the mystifying web of daily experience, and man bleeds himself against the infinite landscape of the universe:

> At first, when death appeared improbable because it had never visited him before, Knight could think of no future, nor of anything connected with his past. He could only look sternly at Nature's treacherous attempt to put an end to him, and strive to thwart her.
>
> From the fact that the cliff formed the inner face of the segment of a huge cylinder, having the sky for a top and the sea for a bottom, which enclosed the bay to the extent of nearly a semicircle, he could see the vertical face curving round on each side of him. He looked far down the facade, and realized more thoroughly how it threatened him. Grimness was in every feature, and to its very bowels the inimical shape was desolation.

By one of those familiar conjunctions of things wherewith the inanimate world baits the mind of man when he pauses in moments of suspense, opposite Knight's eyes was an imbedded fossil, standing forth in low relief from the rock. It was a creature with eyes. The eyes, dead and turned to stone, were even now regarding him. . . . Separated by millions of years in their lives, Knight and this underling seemed to have met in their place of death. It was the instance within reach of his vision of anything that had ever been alive and had had a body to save, as he himself had now.

. . . The immense lapses of time each formation represented had known nothing of the dignity of man. . . . He was to be with the small in his death. . . .

Time closed up like a fan before him. He saw himself at one extremity of the years, face to face with the beginning and all the intermediate centuries simultaneously. Fierce men, clothed in the hides of beasts, and carrying, for defence and attack, huge clubs and pointed spears, rose from the rock, like the phantoms before the doomed Macbeth. They lived in hollows, woods and mud huts—perhaps in caves of the neighbouring rocks. Behind them stood an earlier band. No man was there. Huge elephantine forms, the mastodon, the hippopotamus, the tapir, antelopes of monstrous size, the megatherium, and the myledon—all, for the moment, in juxtaposition. Further back, and overlapped by these, were perched huge billed birds and swinish creatures as large as horses. Still more shadowy were the sinister crocodilian outlines—alligators and other uncouth shapes, culminating in the colossal lizard, the iguanodon. Folded behind were dragon forms and clouds of flying reptiles: still underneath were fishy beings of lower development; and so on, till the lifetime scenes of the fossil confronting him were a present and modern condition of things. These images passed before Knight's inner eye in less

than half a minute, and he was again considering the
actual present. . . . Was Death really stretching out
his hand? The previous sensation, that it was improb-
able he would die, was fainter now.

. . . To those musing weather-beaten West-country
folk who pass the greater part of their days and nights
out of doors, Nature seems to have moods in other
than a poetical sense: predilections for certain deeds
at certain times, without any apparent law to govern
or season to account for them. . . . Man's case is
always that of the prodigal's favourite or the miser's
pensioner. In her unfriendly moments there seems a
feline fun in her tricks, begotten by a foretaste of
her pleasure in swallowing the victim.

Such a way of thinking had been absurd to Knight,
but he began to adopt it now. He was first spitted on
to a rock. New tortures followed. . . .

. . . We are mostly accustomed to look upon all opposition which is not animate as that of the stolid,
inexorable hand of indifference, which wears out the
patience more than the strength. Here, at any rate,
hostility did not assume that slow and sickening form.
It was a cosmic agency, active, lashing, eager for conquest: determination; not an insensate standing in the
way.

. . . It was, as usual, the menacing attitude in which
they [the forces of nature] approached him that magni-
fied their powers.

. . . We colour according to our moods the objects
we survey. . . . [pp. 241–44]

Knight actively experiences the omniscient perspective of
the artist in a way analogous to Hardy's creation of multiple worlds within a single scene; for example, in the
passage at Bede's Inn. But the feeling that Hardy retreated
from the core vision of *A Pair of Blue Eyes* when he wrote
his third novel (only to return to its relentless impulse
later in his career) is reinforced when the narrative curiously pulls back in the final moments of the cliff scene:

> Knight gave up thoughts of life utterly and entirely, and turned to contemplate the Dark Valley and the unknown future beyond. Into the shadowy depths of these speculations we will not follow him. Let it suffice to say what ensued. [p. 245]

Thus, the stifled impulse is buried within the action of the plot; but, as the patterns of all three novels have shown, the dark vision redirects its energy, causing the ingrained tensions of Hardy's fictional world.

Knight, of course, carries his new knowledge with him in his return to life. At the difficult and embarrassed meeting of the three central figures in the tomb of the Luxellians, he utters that awareness as he considers Lady Luxellian's death:

> "Well," said Knight musingly, "let us leave them [the dead]. Such occasions as these seem to compel us to roam outside ourselves, far away from the fragile frame we live in, and to expand till our perception grows so vast that our physical reality bears no sort of proportion to it. We look back upon the weak and minute stem on which this luxuriant growth depends, and ask, Can it be possible that such a capacity has a foundation so small? Must I again return to my daily walk in that narrow cell, a human body, where worldly thoughts can torture me? Do we not?"
>
> "Yes," said Stephen and Elfride.
>
> "One has a sense of wrong, too, that such an appreciative breadth as a sentient being possesses should be committed to the frail casket of a body. What weakens one's intentions regarding the future like the thought of this?" [p. 299]

Knight is the only honest attendant at the meeting; ironically, he is unaware of Elfride and Stephen's attachment, while both "his juniors" (p. 299) know the full story. He is the only one of the three who holds the vision of the cliff, but still does not know the ironic range of his beloved's history in spite of his poisonous suspicions.

Physically not so handsome as either the youthful
architect or the vicar's daughter, the thoroughness
and integrity of Knight illuminated his features with
a dignity not even incipient in the other two. . . .
Elfride, an undeveloped girl, must, perhaps, hardly
be laden with the moral responsibilities which attach
to a man in like circumstances. The charm of woman,
too, lies partly in her subtleness in manners of love.
But if honesty is a virtue in itself, Elfride, having none
of it now, seemed, being for being, scarcely good
enough for Knight. Stephen, though deceptive for no
unworthy purpose, was deceptive after all; and whatever high results grace such strategy if it succeed, it
seldom draws admiration, especially when it fails.
[pp. 299–300]

Hardy is barely euphemistic in his condemnation of Elfride
and Stephen as they stand against Knight. His figure dom-
inates the novel—that he "should have been thus consti-
tuted . . . was the chance of things" (pp. 348–49), so Hardy
tries to assure us. Chance, "of course, is a wholly incorrect
expression, but it serves to acknowledge plainly our ignorance of the cause of each particular variation," at least at
this early point in Hardy's career. Knight's retraction of
his engagement to Elfride, of course, parallels Maybold's
similar action, but his power taps an imaginative source
barely present in the previous novel. Indeed, it is almost
hard to imagine that *A Pair of Blue Eyes* was written
directly after *Under the Greenwood Tree*.

Knight's disappointment in love has "brought him to
the verge of cynicism" (p. 366), that disbelief and readiness
to condemn which often results from such leveling experiences as the revelation of Elfride's childish dishonesty and
the vision on the cliff. Just before the discovery of the
widow Jethway's body in the rubble of the tower (the
tower whose overthrow had been the work of Stephen
Smith), Knight is dimly aware of the complex elements of
the story itself. The interaction of physical environment,

past human events, and the web of emotions is strikingly pronounced in the death of the widow and its consequences. Knight's primary virtue is his ability to embrace the entirety of experience without the help of an illusory veil. "It cankered his heart to think he was confronted by the closest instance of a worse state of things than any he had assumed in the pleasant social philosophy and satire of his essays" (pp. 389–90). He repeats with startling finality the foreboding of the Paddington episode where "the reality [had] so greatly differed from the prefiguring," as he struggles to accept his fate.

> Knight's was a robust intellect, which could escape outside the atmosphere of heart, and perceive that his own love, as well as other people's, could be reduced by change of scene and circumstances. At the same time the perception was a superimposed sorrow:
>
> > "O last regret, regret can die!"
>
> But being convinced that the death of this regret was the best thing for him, he did not long shrink from attempting it. He closed his chambers, suspended his connection with editors, and left London for the Continent. Here we will leave him to wander without purpose, beyond the nominal one of encouraging obliviousness of Elfride. [p. 391]

His struggle represents the battlefield itself, an embodiment of the tensions within these early novels where conceptual illusions are subjected to experience. He had already reached an intellectual awareness of his isolation and its consequences when he entered the novel. It was then that Elfride represented a hope that brought him back momentarily to belief in a world that had existed only as a picture beneath his window. But with the hope shattered, he is forced to reassume his loneliness without illusion.

The shift in emphasis in *A Pair of Blue Eyes* lies within this deep and prolonged gaze into the nature of the intruder himself. Elfride has, of course, been shattered, too;

Stephen has also been hurt, but he is allowed by his nature to find solace in the world of his success. With Elfride's death, the two opposing sensibilities, Knight and Stephen, endure side by side on a scale broader than that of either *Under the Greenwood Tree* or *Far From the Madding Crowd.* The modern man and the representative of traditional order stand together as the result of an ironic dialectic—the man of the present is the former teacher of the innocent, but unknowing, member of the community of the past. The two have been thrown together again at the end of the novel, bound by a common tie to a lover lost forever to them both.

When former mentor meets former pupil in London late in the novel, they are ostensibly on the same level for the first time:

> "Where are you staying?"
> "At the Grosvenor Hotel, Pimlico."
> "So am I." [p. 403]

For Knight, the meeting "had reunited the present with the past" (p. 405), where the irony of full knowledge finally breaks. He sees himself specifically as the victim of circumstance, and the task of acceptance demands his energy again. "It was the first time in Knight's life that he had ever been so entirely the player of a part. And the man he had thus deceived was Stephen, who had docilely looked up to him from youth as a superior of unblemished integrity" (p. 414). Knight has attained the consciousness of the omniscient artist by steps—in his original intellectual attitude, in his philosophical awareness on the cliff, in his emotional resignation to Elfride's irresponsibility, and finally in his recognition of the entire web of events.

Knight is the early version of the later Hardy, the catalyst for a still deeper transformation in the world of the mature novels. It seems that precisely this recognition on Hardy's part caused him to retreat from such a disturbing impulse when he wrote his next book. Knight's secret power was his hold on the artist himself. Maimed but indestruc-

tible, his mutation is Troy. Still, his dark knowledge under-
lies the tension and the abiding wounds in the world of
Far From the Madding Crowd. Hardy stood by his attempt
at suppression on the cliff in his next novel—"Into the
shadowy depths of these speculations we will not follow
him." But the impulse could not be resisted, even in the
so-called idyll of Weatherbury, and it returns to drive the
artist to answer on a still deeper level. It seems that he

> must stand with the average against the exception,
> he must, in his ultimate judgment, represent the in-
> terests of humanity, or the community as a whole,
> and rule out the individual interest.
>
> To do this, however, he must go against himself.
> His private sympathy is always with the individual
> against the community: as is the case with the artist.[11]

The tensions within *Far From the Madding Crowd,*
and even their first whispers in *Under the Greenwood Tree,*
are symptoms of the disturbance; the history of the development of this instinct during Hardy's career as a novelist is
the underlying determinant of the course his fiction was to
follow. "All the phenomena of the formation of symptoms
may be justly described as 'the return of the repressed.'
Their distinguishing characteristic, however, is the far-
reaching distortion to which the returning material has
been subjected as compared with the original." [12]

11. D. H. Lawrence, "Study of Thomas Hardy," in *Selected
Literary Criticism,* p. 183.

12. Sigmund Freud, *Moses and Monotheism,* in *The Standard
Edition of the Complete Psychological Works of Sigmund Freud,* 23:
127. All citations from Freud are from the *Standard Edition* and will
hereafter be indicated by title and volume number alone. The phrase
the return of the repressed first appeared in Freud's published work in
1896 (*Further Remarks on the Neuro-Psychoses of Defense,* 3: 170).

3   *The Return of the Native*

The apparently Darwinian asides in Knight's cliff adventure and at moments in *Far From the Madding Crowd* seemed designed to give expression to a scientific view of nature, assigning an external determinism to a universe that encompasses both the individual and the community. But, as we have seen in Darwin, such a view simply upholds the illusions of a myopic rationalism that refuses to examine its own perceiving lens. By the time he wrote *The Return of the Native,* Hardy seems to have been forced to tackle the initial conflict—between intellect and desire, rational, urban individual and rural community—by reassessing his entire imaginative perspective. The journey into the self has begun: the lens itself must be scrutinized. The question of method becomes correspondingly problematic as the irony of the book, that a native of Wessex has become the rationalist, suggests the involution that is underway.

If we are to believe Albert Guerard's remark that in "every novel we stumble unexpectedly upon signs of the struggle of an undigested idea, an undramatized contrast, an unconcealed and grossly abstract intention . . . [and that] the novels must transcend their theoretical conceptions before they can hope to interest us," [1] then we must ignore the importance of that very struggle. For, in his early attempts at fiction, Hardy brought the individual intellect to bear on the community, and, sensing difficulties, moved to examine both the nature of community and of the individual. We have seen the implications of the kind of rationalism embraced by Leslie Stephen; Hardy, as an artist who was tremendously drawn to rational modes of

1. Albert Guerard, *Thomas Hardy*, pp. 63, 65.

thought, must have felt the need to search beyond the intellect. And while it seems that he retained a conscious belief in the faculty of reason (even if it led only to despair), his imagination was still free to move elsewhere. Yet the deeper he drove to the recesses of his characters, tracing the minute details of their inner lives in an attempt to resolve the conflict, the more his rational propensities rebelled at being sentenced to silence. His "churchiness," or sense of community, had been destroyed by Knight just as his religious orthodoxy had been reduced to ruins.

At about the time *The Return of the Native* was completed, Hardy recorded two reflections that begin to suggest the outline of this maturer period:

> "April–Note. A Plot, or Tragedy, should arise from the gradual closing in of a situation that comes of ordinary human passions, prejudices, and ambitions, by reason of the characters taking no trouble to ward off the disastrous events produced by the said passions, prejudices, and ambitions.
>
> "The advantages of the letter-system of telling a story (passing over the disadvantages) are that, hearing what one side has to say, you are led constantly to the imagination of what the other side must be feeling, and at last are anxious to know if the other side does really feel what you imagine. [*Life,* p. 120]

Here, he places responsibility directly with his characters, invoking no determinism from without—the implication is, instead, that whatever determinants exist within a narrative are "by reason of the characters [themselves] taking no trouble to ward off the disastrous events produced"; what happens to them is a function of their own constitutions. By the "advantages of the letter-system" of storytelling, he seems to reaffirm our understanding of the poetics of the early novels: that the world of a novel becomes alive only when events become important to the characters and, as a result, affect the community in which they move.

An entry of the same month rounds out Hardy's intel-

lectual recognition of the growing dramatic processes now
refining the modes already followed in his earlier work:

> "April 22. The method of Boldini, the painter of
> "The Morning Walk" in the French Gallery two or
> three years ago . . . —of Hobbema, in his view of a
> road with formal lopped trees and flat tame scenery—
> is that of infusing emotion into the baldest external
> objects either by the presence of a human figure among
> them, or by mark of some human connection with
> them.
>
> "This accords with my feeling about, say, Heidel-
> berg and Baden *versus* Scheveningen—as I wrote at
> the beginning of *The Return of the Native*—that
> the beauty of association is entirely superior to the
> beauty of aspect, and a beloved relative's old battered
> tankard to the finest Greek vase. Paradoxically put,
> it is to see the beauty in ugliness." [*Life*, pp. 120–21]

His concern with the relation between landscape and the
human figure assumes a form which reveals the needs that
have wrought refinements in his poetics. The meaning of
his earlier remark now becomes even more significant:
"The writer's problem is, how to strike a balance between
the uncommon and the ordinary . . . [while] . . . human
nature must never be made abnormal. . . . The uncommonness must be in the events, not in the characters." At
the same time, "[t]ragedy . . . should arise from the gradual closing in of a situation that comes of ordinary human
passions" and ordinary human weaknesses in response to
those passions. But Hardy stresses, too, that the "poetry of
a scene varies with the minds of the perceivers." Thus
landscape, in the sense of the relation between external
scenery or objects and human figures, becomes the most
natural mode for mediating the demands of his poetics.
The "beauty of association" can be used as a means of defining character and event from a character's perspective.
Even with some intellectual awareness of these possibilities,

though, Hardy still uses landscape in only a limited way at this point in his career: as a reflection, by simile or analogy, of his characters' moods and natures. As his substantive concerns move away from a community-oriented perspective (where individuals are seen in terms of a society, as either members or intruders) toward the perspective of the individual himself, his imaginative methods become correspondingly refined. Hardy's changing use of landscape is important both as a mediator between human community and nature and as a means of creating individual consciousness. *The Return of the Native* furnishes the richest example of this brooding transitional period, as the universe of the early novels moves toward the vision of the later Hardy.

The opening chapter of the novel turns on the suspended transition from day to night on Egdon Heath. It is the counterpart in external, inanimate nature to the suspended moments between waking and sleeping in individual consciousness described in the opening chapter of Proust's *Remembrance of Things Past*. The comparison is strikingly suggestive of a direction Hardy was just beginning to pursue at the time he wrote *The Return of the Native*. In a book that appeared the year before the first volume of Proust's work, Freud's *Totem and Taboo* (1912), the significance of our comparison finds apt conceptual expression: "owing to the projection outwards of internal perceptions, primitive men arrived at a picture of the external world which we, with our intensified conscious perception, have now to translate back into psychology." "We are thus prepared to find that primitive man transposed the structural conditions of his own mind into the external world; and we may attempt to reverse the process and put back into the human mind what animism teaches as to the nature of things." [2]

2. Sigmund Freud, *Totem and Taboo*, 13: 64, 91. Freud's insight is applicable to the changes that took place in the form of the novel between Hardy and Proust: "Radical changes take place in the . . .

In fact, precisely at this transitional point of its
nightly roll into darkness the great and particular
glory of the Egdon waste began, and nobody could be
said to understand the heath who had not been there
at such a time. It could best be felt when it could not
clearly be seen . . . then, and only then, did it tell
its true tale . . . the sombre stretch of rounds and
hollows seemed to rise and meet the evening gloom
in pure sympathy, the heath exhaling darkness as
rapidly as the heavens precipitated it. And so the obscurity in the air and the obscurity in the land closed
together in a black fraternization toward which each
advanced half-way.

The place became full of a watchful intentness now;
for when other things sank brooding to sleep the heath
appeared slowly to awake and listen. Every night its
Titanic form seemed to await something; but it had
waited thus, unmoved, during so many centuries,
through the crises of so many things, that it could only
be imagined to await one last crisis—the final overthrow. [pp. 3–4]

For a long time I used to go to bed early. Sometimes,
when I had put out my candle, my eyes would close
so quickly that I had not even time to say "I'm going
to sleep." And half an hour later the thought that it
was time to go to sleep would awaken me. . . . [An]
impression would persist for some moments after I
was awake; it did not disturb my mind, but it lay like
scales upon my eyes and prevented them from register-
ing the fact that the candle was no longer burning.
Then it would begin to seem unintelligible, as the
thoughts of a former existence must be to a reincarnate
spirit. . . .

---

novel in the fifty years between the publication of *Middlemarch*
(1871) and *Ulysses* (1922), greater than those of either the preceding
or subsequent half-centuries" (Peter K. Garrett, *Scene and Symbol
from George Eliot to James Joyce*, p. 1).

When a man is asleep, he has in a circle round him the chain of the hours, the sequence of the years, the order of the heavenly host. Instinctively, when he awakes, he looks to these, and in an instant reads off his own position on the earth's surface and the amount of time that has elapsed during his slumbers; but this ordered procession is apt to grow confused and to break its ranks.[3]

In *The Return of the Native,* Hardy's landscape becomes personalized to a much greater degree than at any point in his earlier novels. And, as if to substantiate the feeling that the heath itself represents the explicit description of the psyche Proust was to achieve, the artist tells us that "[h]aggard Egdon appealed to a subtler and scarcer instinct, to a more recently learnt emotion, than that which responds to the sort of beauty called charming and fair" (p. 5). The separation between the perceiver and scene, of course, still remains; but an affinity between the perceptive sensibility and the nature of the world it beholds is clearly suggested. Hardy's early diary entry has already suggested this tendency: "The poetry of a scene varies with the minds of the perceivers. Indeed, it does not lie in the scene at all"; "the beauty of association" that he notes at the time of his completion of the novel confirms the fact that he was also moving consciously in this direction. The passage in the novel to which he refers in the note takes on added meaning in the context of the landscape:

human souls may find themselves in closer and closer harmony with external things wearing a somberness distasteful to our race when it was young. The time seems near, if it has not actually arrived, when the chastened sublimity of a moor, a sea, or a mountain, will be all of nature that is absolutely in keeping with the moods of the more thinking among mankind. And ultimately, to the commonest tourist, spots like Iceland may become what the vineyards and myrtle-gar-

3. Marcel Proust, *Swann's Way* (New York, 1956), pp. 3, 6.

dens of South Europe are to him now; and Heidelberg
and Baden be passed unheeded as he hastens from the
Alps to the sand-dunes of Scheveningen. [p. 5]

As Egdon takes on symbolic proportions, he moves further:

Intensity was more usually reached by way of the
brilliant, and such a sort of intensity was often arrived
at during winter darkness, tempests, and mists. Then
Egdon was aroused to reciprocity; for the storm was
its lover and the wind its friend. Then it became the
home of strange phantoms; *and it was found to be the
hitherto unrecognized original of those wild regions
of obscurity which are vaguely felt to be compassing
us about in midnight dreams of flight and disaster,
and are never thought of after the dream till revived
by scenes like this.* [pp. 5–6; my italics]

The aspect of the heath in Hardy's imagination becomes
"the hitherto unrecognized *original* of those wild regions
of obscurity" glimpsed in our most terrible dreams. It is
the bedrock of man's essence, but the tension inherent in
his imagination holds the language to analogy, just short
of identity:

It was at present a place perfectly accordant with
man's nature—neither ghastly, hateful, nor ugly: neither commonplace, unmeaning, nor tame; but, like
man, slighted and enduring; and withal singularly
colossal and mysterious in its swarthy monotony. . . .
It had a lonely face, suggesting tragical possibilities.
. . . The untameable, Ishmaelitish thing that Egdon
now was it always had been. Civilization was its enemy. [p. 6]

But momentarily he is set free to describe the deepest
stratum of the scene in its resemblance to man's nature
(the topographical language is strangely akin to Freud's
images of the psyche):

To recline on a stump of thorn in the central valley
of Egdon, between afternoon and night, as now, where

the eye could reach nothing of the world outside the summits and shoulders of heathland which filled the whole circumference of its glance, and to know that everything around and underneath had been from prehistoric times as unaltered as the stars overhead, gave ballast to the mind adrift on change, and harassed by the irrepressible New. The great inviolate place had an ancient permanence which the sea cannot claim. [pp. 6–7]

Here lies the realm of instinct, that which alone remains natural in man—"the hitherto unrecognized original." An implicit contrast is made in the passage between the central valley, suggesting the unconscious id whose peaks and crags prohibit converse with the demands of the external world, and the conscious mind, a faculty distinct from this valley, "adrift on change," "harassed by the irrepressible New," which must come to recognize that the central valley is its true home.

As the chapter closes, the suspended vision is brought into relation with the external world. Hardy discloses the existence of "an aged highway," the only aspect of the landscape that marks man's conscious intentions within the wilderness. Before a human figure appears on the scene, then, the artist has established a new fictional universe. It is a world where both the impulses of the conscious individual and the community are allowed expression. Unlike *A Pair of Blue Eyes*, where Knight predominates because of the rawness of his fresh discovery, and *Far From the Madding Crowd*, where that impulse was suppressed with the result of an infected community, Hardy is now ready to confront the struggle between the two worlds as he builds upon a new foundation.

Just as the first chapter of *The Return of the Native* establishes a psychological landscape against which the action of the novel takes place, the first book of the novel, "The Three Women," forms a prologue to the real plot, which does not really begin until Clym appears in the second book. It announces the capacities of man (conscious, acting man) within the limits of mortal existence: a rumbling underworld of dark passion, "the central valley," weighing against humanity from below, and an equally unknown and threatening world without, including "Civilization . . . its enemy." While at first the landscape of the opening chapter seems only static, its dynamic nature is revealed in that "black fraternization" of sky and earth, light and dark. The first chapter is a metaphor for the human mind; within it, or against it, Hardy's characters play out their lives.

As if the presence of tension were not perceptible already, the title of the second chapter states the obvious: "Humanity Appears on the Scene Hand in Hand with Trouble." The landscape now changes from symbol to reality, as the first human figure, old Captain Vye, makes his way along the road through the wilderness. As soon as Hardy describes him, we see yet another human figure on the road, but this time from the first character's point of view. Thus, in two strokes, Hardy moves, first, from a symbolic overview to a more realistic mode, and then directly into the world of men. But the impression of the first chapter remains; the human world has been infused with the atmosphere of the opening pages on Egdon, as we see Venn through Vye's eyes: "It was the single atom of life that the scene contained, and it only served to render the general loneliness more evident" (p. 8). That Hardy grants the perceiving eye to a single character (if only for one sentence) testifies to the meaning of the movement of these first pages.

At this transitional hour "there was that in the condition of the heath itself which resembled protracted halting and dubiousness" (p. 12), a condition betraying the tension of the dynamic elements that have been suggested so far. Mystery and intrigue have already figured in the action, too—the woman in Venn's van, the presence of the reddleman himself, and Eustacia's form upon the hill. When the rustics group at the spot abandoned by Eustacia, we learn that she "had no relation to the forms who had taken her place" (p. 14). There is irony and a leaden foreshadowing in Hardy's formalized response to her departure:

> The imagination of the observer clung by preference to that vanished, solitary figure, as to something more interesting, more important, more likely to have a history worth knowing than these new-comers, and unconsciously regarded them as intruders. [p. 14]

Hardy betrays his sympathies early—Eustacia is the intruder upon the heath, the danger to the community; but we already feel that the forces of nature are in secret alliance with her. The barrenness of the soil on the heath exposes the community: we can see the true outlines of society more easily here than in the richer agricultural areas of Wessex. With the bonfires ablaze, the community functions at its most primitive level to the discerning spiritual eye:

> In the heath's barrenness to the farmer lay its fertility to the historian. There had been no obliteration because there had been no tending.
>
> It was as if the bonfire-makers were standing in some radiant upper story of the world, detached from and independent of the dark stretches below. The heath down there was now a vast abyss, and no longer a continuation of what they stood on; for their eyes, adapted to the blaze, could see nothing of the deeps beyond its influence. [p. 17]

With this view comes a response:

> Moreover, to light a fire is the instinctive and resistant act of man when, at the winter ingress, the curfew is sounded throughout Nature. It indicates a spontaneous, Promethean rebelliousness against the fiat that this recurrent season shall bring foul time, cold darkness, misery and death. Black chaos comes, and the fettered gods of the earth say, Let there be light. [pp. 17–18]

And since the poetry of a scene issues from the nature of its perception, Hardy recalls the stark outlines:

Those whom Nature had depicted as merely quaint became grotesque, the grotesque became preternatural; for all was in extremity. [p. 18]

This is November on the heath, when the land betrays its starkest qualitites and man is called upon to preserve the species; it seems that Hardy sees winter as the truest expression of the heath since in its barrenness "lay its fertility to the historian." Man's Promethean rebelliousness at this symbolic fire-time reveals, not his conquest of nature, but his blindness to "the dark stretches below," the mental accompaniment to his material need for warmth. Fire is civilization, "Civilization [Egdon's] enemy": the perverse Platonic overtones in the inhabitants' adaptation to the ironic and reverse truth of their fires evoke a seething picture of the dynamics of human society and nature. Paradoxically, in answering his needs man blinds himself to his own nature (given the dual function of the heath as a symbol of man's unconscious and as actual physical nature). The potential for the destruction of the community no longer lies with an external interference; it is latent within the society itself. The seeds of its destruction lurk within its blindness to its own nature.

The community, however, can remain stable as long as it huddles by its fires, ignorant of "the dark stretches below." In an article on the Dorsetshire laborer in *Longman's Magazine* in July 1883, Hardy was to write:

It is among such communities as these that happiness will find her last refuge upon earth, since it is among them that a perfect insight into the conditions of existence will be longest postponed.[4]

The potential threat to order, however, lies in the possibility of a consciousness of the true power of "the vast abyss below." Such a consciousness may be evoked by a perspective that is not bound to the community. While an intrusive intelligence was seen as the cause of infection in the

4. Quoted in Rutland, *Thomas Hardy,* p. 89.

early novels, it now becomes only the catalyst for self-recognition, "the mind adrift on change." The "irrepressible New" can only be awareness of "the hitherto unrecognized original." This is the point from which a formulation of Hardy's sense of "modern" must begin: the extension of consciousness from the deceptive light of the most newly built fire to the surrounding territories of darkness.

But a conflict lies at the very heart of the discovery: *all* fires must be extinguished in order to learn to see in the darkness. The state of suspension between the extinction of the fires and the ability to move in the night is the ground of the struggle; it is the abyss into which Hardy's major characters must now descend. Their journeys and their fates, once they confront "the hitherto unrecognized," comprise tragedy. With Hardy's next major work, *The Mayor of Casterbridge,* we shall see a full statement of this kind of tragedy—"modern" tragedy—when the confrontation occurs within the mind (the wish as deed) without the necessity of acting. But because the artist himself is groping in the darkness, Henchard's tragedy must still be *communicated* to us primarily by his actions, while the dynamics of the tragic individual himself, as we shall see, are internal. In spite of the suggestive opening of *The Return of the Native,* the novel holds back from fulfilling itself in this direction, and we must wait for *The Mayor* to see the fuller design.

Hardy focuses more closely on Eustacia in the first book than on any other character. She returns to the barrow after the rustics have departed: "There she stood still, around her stretching the vast night atmosphere, whose incomplete darkness in comparison with the total darkness of the heath below it might have represented a venial beside a mortal sin" (p. 59). In spite of her hatred of the heath and of her situation, it seems that Eustacia is at one with the symbolic proportions of the landscape. As if to confirm a suggested analogy, Hardy has told us that "[p]ersons with any weight of character carry, like planets, their atmospheres along with them in their orbits" (p. 35). Because Eustacia is

an outsider by temperament as well as by history, we sense
an irony in the remark that "the observer clung by preference
to [her] vanished, solitary figure" on the hill, and "unconsciously regarded [the rustics themselves] as outsiders."
What Guerard calls "the progressive domination of nature
by temperament" [5] in the development of the novels ("The
poetry of a scene varies with the minds of the perceivers")
describes both the artist's consciousness and the possibilities
of Eustacia's: precisely because her consciousness is predisposed to recognize "the hitherto unrecognized original," she is the catalyst for the possibility of the community's infection. "Such views of life were to some extent
the natural begettings of her situation upon her nature"
(p. 81). Through Clym, she will infect the community in
that she will force it to realize the possibility of its destruction from within. The actual germ of the downfall of the
old order is latent within the community itself—it becomes
active when an exterior consciousness calls it into movement.[6]

For Eustacia, her "woman's brain had authorized what
it could not regulate" (p. 62); her sighs are "but another
phrase of the same discourse" as the winds (p. 61). In her
confrontation with her first lover, Wildeve, she speaks of
"a strange warring [that] takes place in [her] mind" (p. 72).
Her consciousness of her own microcosmic struggle is en-
riched by Hardy's loaded metaphors: "Whenever a flash of
reason darted like an electric light upon her lover—as it
sometimes would—and showed his imperfections, she shiv-
ered. . . . But it was over in a second, and she loved on"
(pp. 73–74). The definitive modern intellectual tool, "reason," and its symbolic product, "an electric light," bespeak
her own "bonfire." Because she is ever willing to abandon
its light, her choice is clear. She is likened to a pagan
goddess:

5. Guerard, p. 77.
6. This pattern changes as the subjects of the later novels change,
from a focus on the community to the individual. Its final version
occurs in *Jude the Obscure*.

But celestial imperiousness, love, wrath, and fervour had proved to be somewhat thrown away on netherward Egdon. Her power was limited, and the consciousness of this limitation had biased her development. Egdon was her Hades, and since coming there she had imbibed much of what was dark in its tone, though inwardly and eternally unreconciled thereto. [p. 77]

The native inhabitants fear that she is a witch precisely because she poses a danger to the community. Just as "all was extremity" on the heath early in the book, there is "no middle distance in her perspective" (p. 78) either:

Eustacia had got beyond the vision of some marriage of inexpressible glory; yet, though her emotions were in full vigour, she cared for no meaner union. Thus we see her in a strange state of isolation. To have lost the godlike conceit that we may do what we will, and not to have acquired a homely zest for doing what we can, shows a grandeur of temper which cannot be objected to in the abstract, for it denotes a mind that, though disappointed, forswears compromise. But, if congenial to philosophy, it is apt to be dangerous to the commonwealth. In a world where doing means marrying, and the commonwealth is one of hearts and hands, the same peril attends the condition. [p. 81]

. . . As far as social ethics were concerned, Eustacia approached the savage state, though in emotion she was all the while an epicure. She had advanced to the secret recesses of sensuousness, yet had hardly crossed the threshold of conventionality. [p. 109]

Eustacia's key position in the plot is now clear: she acts, of course, within the limits which have just been defined in her character and which correspond to the contours of the landscape early in the novel. That "strange warring" in her mind is a reflection of Egdon at twilight; that "black fraternization" suspends her between a refusal to use light and an equal refusal to explore the darkness. She is not quite a tragic character herself: but, given her relationship with Clym, she may throw the community, through him, into the abyss. Her refusals become her choices because of that forswearing of compromise, which, "if congenial to philosophy, . . . is apt to be dangerous to the commonwealth." She will not act upon her knowledge of the world within ("the secret recesses" to which she has advanced) and, thus, "had hardly crossed the threshold of conventionality"—but the visitation of that knowledge works upon all who come into contact with her. She has seen "the irrepressible New," but will not, or cannot, recognize it in herself. She feels the struggle within, but responds consciously only to her known, superficial desires.

Clym and Eustacia represent the two new ways in which Hardy tries to deal with his imaginative impulses in *The Return of the Native*. The lovers are both Knight's heirs: they combine his two most dangerous qualities, an intrusion into the community and a rational intelligence. But, having gone beyond the frontier of reason, Hardy has discovered a new counterpart to the inquiring (and now idealized) intellect, an alliance between natural forces and the passions of a woman. Where in the early novels, the individual's reason and the emotional bonds of the community formed the tension, the conflict has now shifted to a deeper level. With the infection of the community by reason, Hardy has begun to search for the limits of the reasoning capacity itself: Eustacia informs Clym, and both inform the dissolution of the strength of the ordered society.

After the wild, poetic strains of his descriptions of the heath and of Eustacia in the first book of the novel, Hardy's introduction of Yeobright allows the real action to begin. The strength of the lovers' union is defined in a perfect symbolic paradox that reveals the unity of the novel: "Take all the varying hates felt by Eustacia Vye towards the heath, and translate them into loves, and you have the heart of Clym" (p. 205). While the statement is definitive, it betrays Hardy's not infrequent reliance on a formula-like manner of conceptualization or summary. But in the

very betrayal of such stylistic weaknesses, one of the central
tensions in the imaginative universe is revealed. Indeed,
the stylistic differences between Hardy's poetic language in
describing the heath and Eustacia, and his leaden, conceptual, prosaic rendering of Clym, both express the artist's
varying sympathies with his characters and the translation
of that tension into other dualities issuing from the same
source. Consider these descriptions of Clym against the
earlier portraits of Eustacia:

> To one of middle age the countenance was that of
> a young man, though a youth might hardly have seen
> any necessity for the term of immaturity. But it was
> really one of those faces which convey less the idea of
> so many years as its age than of so much experience
> as its store. The number of their years may have been
> adequately summed up Jared, Mahalaleel, and the
> rest of the antediluvians, but the age of a modern man
> is to be measured by the intensity of his history.
>
> The face was well shaped, even excellently. But the
> mind within was beginning to use it as a mere waste
> tablet whereon to trace its idiosyncrasies as they devel-
> oped themselves. The beauty here visible would in
> no long time be ruthlessly overrun by its parasite,
> thought. [p. 161]

> . . . He already showed that thought is a disease
> of flesh, and indirectly bore evidence that ideal physical
> beauty is incompatible with emotional development
> and a full recognition of the coil of things. Mental
> luminousness must be fed with the oil of life, even
> though there is already a physical need for it; and
> the pitiful sight of two demands on one supply was
> just showing itself here.
>
> As for his look, it was a natural cheerfulness striving
> against depression from without, and not quite succeed-
> ing. The look suggested isolation, but revealed some-
> thing more. As is usual with bright natures, the deity

> that lies ignominiously chained within an ephemeral human carcass shone out of him like a ray.
>
> The effect upon Eustacia was palpable. [p. 162]

Hardy's poetic rendering of Eustacia and prosaic presentation of Clym are complemental in terms of the view they grant us of the creating mind behind the fiction. Style becomes meaning and structure betrays content: Hardy as artist sympathizes with Eustacia and, even more, with the narrative consciousness he exhibits in the opening pages of the novel; on the other hand, the sympathies of Hardy the conceptualist and rational thinker lie with Clym and with his account of Yeobright's intellectual aspect. He has already called him "a modern man" whose age "is to be measured by the intensity of his history," like the heath's. It is precisely Clym's intellectual awareness of what Eustacia feels but cannot recognize that signifies his intellectual "modernism":

> He was a John the Baptist who took ennoblement rather than repentance for his text. Mentally he was in a provincial future, that is, he was in many points abreast with the central town thinkers of his date. Much of this development he may have owed to his studious life in Paris, where he had become acquainted with ethical systems popular at this time.
>
> In consequence of this relatively advanced position, Yeobright might have been called unfortunate. The rural world was not ripe for him. [pp. 203–04]

But here the conflicting tendencies within Hardy's own mind appear in their reflection in the imaginative universe: the rural world of Egdon Heath, "away from comparisons" (p. 123), contains all that the most advanced conceptual minds of the age following Hardy's could recognize.[7] It is his *dramatic* consciousness that approximates the next gen-

7. The implication is that the conceptual apparatus of Hardy's intellectual environment did not provide an outlet for his mature fictional insights. With Freud (Proust, Joyce, Lawrence, etc.), the new equipment was being built.

eration's concepts, both in the scenes of the heath and of Eustacia. But with his introduction of Clym, the idealized intellectual, Hardy's own efforts at thought (which, as an artist, he has condemned as "a disease of flesh") seem to take precedence over his dramatic impulses. Indeed, Hardy himself describes precisely this tension in an aside during one of his descriptions of Clym:

> When standing before certain men the philosopher regrets that thinkers are but perishable tissue, the artist that perishable tissue has to think. Thus to deplore, each from his point of view, the mutually destructive interdependence of spirit and flesh would have been instinctive with these in critically observing Yeobright. [p. 162]

And so it is the case with Hardy himself. Following his account of Clym's urbane "modernism," he writes:

> If anyone knew the heath well, it was Clym. He was permeated with its scenes, with its substance, and with its odours. He might be said to be its product. His eyes had first opened thereon; with its appearance all the first images of his memory were mingled. [p. 205]

As the model of the juxtaposition, then: "Much of [his intellectual] development *he may have owed to* his studious life in Paris, where he had become acquainted with the ethical systems popular at the time"; while *"He might be said to be* its [the heath's] product" (my italics). Hardy goes far in his attempt to dramatize Clym's harmony with his native home, especially in his role as furze-cutter, when even his mother cannot distinguish him from the landscape ("He was a brown spot in the midst of an expanse of olive-green gorse, and nothing more," p. 298; and, when his mother sees him, he "appeared as a mere parasite of the heath," p. 328). That Hardy uses the metaphor *parasite* as a description both of thought (p. 161) and of Clym's work upon the heath (p. 328) evidences the degree to which Clym's characterization touches upon central conflicts in the artist's imagination. The creation of Yeobright seems strained, almost artificial—especially in contrast to the flowing, breathing Eustacia.

The rustics exhibit distrust toward Clym, in spite of their long affection for him, when he reveals his plans to establish a school on the heath. He stirs essentially the same fear in the natives that prompts their condemnation of Eustacia as a witch. Clym's announced rational desire is "an attempt to disturb a sequence to which humanity has been long accustomed" (p. 204)—namely, ignorance of itself. Again, he functions as the self-conscious expression of the dramatic impulses brought to life in Eustacia. As if to emphasize Clym's function as her conceptual counterpart, Christian appears with the news that "Susan Nunsuch had pricked Miss Vye with a long stockingneedle" (p. 209) in church directly after Yeobright's attempt to explain to his mother that he wants to teach men "how to breast the misery they are born to" (p. 207).

Clym's return markedly affects Eustacia's life: "her colourless inner world would before night become as animated as water under a microscope" (p. 127). Clym's relationship with her resembles the "propagandists" that Hardy describes as succeeding "because the doctrine they bring into form is that which their listeners have for some time felt without being able to shape" (p. 204). We are told, too, that Clym's mind is not well proportioned, just as Eustacia's is not, although for different reasons. Yeobright seeks to help his fellow men even at the risk of sacrificing himself; while Eustacia claims: "I have not much love for my fellow-creatures. Sometimes I quite hate them" (p. 219).

Hardy's artistic sympathy lies secretly with Eustacia and the early vision of the heath. "In each of these instances Hardy's sympathy, which was the great source of his creative energy, proved more powerful than his clearly defined intentions; his characters did not escape him, but they did escape his didactic view of their problems." [8] The "electric light" of Clym's intellect becomes but another community

8. Guerard, p. 70.

fire that literally blinds him to the darkness—he impairs his eyesight by reading—thought, the "disease of flesh." Just as the community is susceptible to collapse once its fiery illusions have been extinguished, so Clym's passion for Eustacia breaks down Egdon's resistance to the germ within its own nature. Clym's rupture with his mother because of his marriage symbolizes the drift of the action; it is noteworthy, too, that Mrs. Yeobright has been concerned with social forms and conventions throughout the novel. Yeobright's idealized intellectualism is worthless (Hardy as thinker) when confronted with the living force behind his ideas in Eustacia (Hardy as artist).

> If it were not that man is much stronger in feeling than in thought, the Wessex novels would be sheer rubbish, as they are already in parts. . . .
>
> But it is not as a metaphysician that one must consider Hardy. He makes a poor show there. For nothing is so pitiable as his clumsy efforts to push events into line with his theory of being. . . .
>
> His feeling, his instinct, his sensuous understanding is, however, apart from his metaphysic, very great and deep, deeper than that, perhaps, of any other English novelist. Putting aside his metaphysic, which must always obtrude when he thinks of people, and turning to the earth, to landscape, then he is true to himself.[9]

The logic of plot is identical to the implications of the logic of character. Eustacia acts against Clym's wishes at the crucial moment of his mother's visit to Anglebury. Eustacia consequently assumes responsibility while Clym suffers; finally, when she receives punishment, he must endure the pain. The full flush of their love occurs during summer on the heath, that deceptive time when Egdon appears gorgeous, but winter is sure to return to reveal

9. D. H. Lawrence, "Study of Thomas Hardy," in *Selected Literary Criticism*, p. 189.

once again the bare outlines of man and nature. Almost exactly at the middle of the novel, Hardy describes the landscape against which Clym and Eustacia's love grows "to oppressiveness" (p. 231):

> Everything before them was on a perfect level. . . . [p. 244]

> . . . Clym watched her as she retired towards the sun . . . As he watched, the dead flat of the scenery overpowered him, though he was fully alive to the beauty of that untarnished early summer green which was worn for the nonce by the poorest blade. There was something in its oppressive horizontality which too much reminded him of the arena of life; it gave him a sense of bare equality with, and no superiority to, a single living thing under the sun. [p. 245]

The seasons, the landscape, and man have moved from the winter of the opening of the novel to this "arena of life": but an overpowering heat pervades this deceptive openness and, like the passion of the lovers, takes Mrs. Yeobright's life.

Bound to the heath, bound to each other, Clym and Eustacia work out the contradictions of a fatal dialectic: her forswearing of compromise, "congenial to philosophy, . . . is apt to be dangerous to the commonwealth"; she feels and acts and is the catalyst for the turn of the action. Clym thinks, but remains blind to the true mysteries of the heath, like his mother and the rustics. Artist triumphs over thinker as flesh triumphs over spirit. The battle of "the mutually destructive interdependence of spirit and flesh" in the mind of the author can only bind itself to the invocation of the opening pages of the novel: "the hitherto unrecognized original" becomes "the return of the repressed" and informs the imaginative universe in deed. Clym, while intellectually harassed by "the irrepressible New," still cannot feel the recognition of its power because he was born to the heath and, as a result, must remain blind to it. Eustacia, the intruder, surveys Egdon from the hilltop and unthinkingly responds to its darkest impulses in her feelings and actions.

Clym's view of the heath, especially as an "arena of life" and as an open vista of apparently clear consciousness, is a function of his own perceptions; just as Eustacia's kinship to the wild and craglike winter heath of the first book draws the firmest lines of her character. Thomasin and Venn's ability to make their way about the heath as natives, without fear and with only their conscious intentions directing them, reflect at a distance Clym's original nature. Had Yeobright never gone to Paris, he would not have been attractive to Eustacia—nor, in metaphorical translation, would he ever have become her conceptual counterpart. Thus, Hardy's imagination is impelled to creation by necessary tensions: the electric light of reason, and thought, a disease of the flesh (Clym), are ranged against the hitherto unrecognized original of the central valley, the secret recesses of sensuousness (Eustacia).

The importance of *The Return of the Native* lies in its discovery that the source of the community's potential for downfall lies within the deep recesses of the nature of society itself. The device of the outside intruder has become a catalyst rather than a cause. The marriage between Venn and Thomasin at the end of the novel is as false as Clym's becoming a preacher; as Hardy joins the devil's party, each new insight triggers such repressive responses. With his next book, however, a sustained vision will finally emerge from the combat of the past.

4   *The Mayor of Casterbridge*

With *The Mayor of Casterbridge,* we arrive at a full statement of Hardy's universe. "The story is more particularly a
study of one man's deeds and character than, perhaps, any
other of those included in my Exhibition of Wessex life"
(author's preface). The definitive statement of Hardy's
achievement in *The Mayor,* a pronouncement of central
importance to the body of his fiction, occurs directly after
Donald Farfrae's crucial dismissal by Henchard and the
Scotsman's establishment of his own business:

> But most probably luck had little to do with it.
> Character is Fate, said Novalis, and Farfrae's character
> was just the reverse of Henchard's, who might not in-
> aptly be described as Faust has been described—as a
> vehement gloomy being who had quitted the ways of
> vulgar men without light to guide him on a better
> way. [p. 131]

That the dialectic of complementary characters would be
the logic of Hardy's mature poetics was decided by *The
Return of the Native.* In *The Mayor,* that discovery is recognized by the artist to the point of explicit statement and,
as a result, directs the movement of the entire work. The
passage develops the rich metaphor of the bonfires on the
heath and its modern translation as the "electric light" of
reason in its direct relation to the structure of the novel.
We suggested in the last chapter that "modern" consciousness in Hardy begins with the suspended moment between
the individual's extinguishing of the self-blinding communal fires and his ensuing need, or willingness, to find his
way in the darkness. It was here, too, that Hardy betrayed
his true sympathy—that of the artist, not the thinker.

The Return of the Native showed that the old order is helpless before the new because of an inner defect, not simply because of external interference. The narrative of *The Mayor* is "the steadily developed decline of a protagonist who incarnates the older order, and whose decline is linked, more and more clearly, with an inner misdirection, an inner weakness." [1] Hardy's advance in his tale of Casterbridge lies in the recognition that the energy diffused in *The Return* because of the artist's residual hesitations now becomes concentrated in the person of Michael Henchard. The impulses of the earlier book that found expression in the psychological, symbolic landscape of the heath are now contained within a single individual. The backdrop of the psyche represented by the heath was the rugged canvas of the mind upon which the two conflicting, yet inexorably linked, instincts in the artist's imagination were expressed: first, in the oppressive love of inseparable counterparts; and then, in the mortal combat of that "mutually destructive interdependence." After his exploration of the individual in *The Mayor,* Hardy will proceed to examine the isolated ego (the self-alienation discovered in Henchard) and its origins in an investigation of the individual and society in *Tess* and *Jude.*

Hardy's diary entry for April 1878, which helped to define the view that determinism exists within the world of character rather than as a force external to man, revealed the deepest contours of *The Return;* it may also serve to clarify the universe of *The Mayor:* "A Plot, or Tragedy, should arise from the gradual closing in of a situation that comes of ordinary human passions, prejudices, and ambitions, and by reason of the characters taking no trouble to ward off the disastrous events [so] produced." With Henchard, the case is intensified, and the idea of "taking no trouble" becomes itself the issue of an internal struggle within the individual. The working-out of "Character is Fate" provides a detailed view of the inner determinants as

1. John Holloway, "Hardy's Major Fiction," in *The Charted Mirror,* pp. 99–100.

they express themselves in events. But of course the novel is not an illustration of that concept. In fact, the power of Hardy's dramatic impulses is so overwhelming here that even his present ability to use symbolic landscape breaks down before the bare emotion of character itself, as we shall see late in the book: "To this he had come after a time of emotional darkness of which the adjoining woodland shade afforded inadequate illustration" (p. 330). The primacy of plot, the dialectic of character (now both between men and within the individual alone) and the events this dialectic produces, return with full force after the artist's modal explorations in *The Return*. The year after the publication of *The Mayor*, Hardy wrote: "July 14. It is the on-going—i.e., the 'becoming'—of the world that produces its sadness. If the world stood still at a felicitous moment there would be no sadness in it" (*Life*, p. 202). The movement of character through narrative produces events at the same time that it reveals the meaning of Hardy's method. The narrative trajectory [2] brings us, time and again, to the suspended moment between the extinction of illusory guiding fires and the wandering in the darkness.[3] Those moments of darkness occur when the artist, and, progressively, Henchard, recognize that

> The unconscious is the true psychic reality; in its inner nature it is just as much unknown to us as the reality of the external world, and it is just as imperfectly communicated to us by the data of consciousness as is the external world by the reports of our sense-organs.[4]

The forces in Henchard's own nature drive him to action. Robert Heilman observes that the "shock of realization that he has actually sold his wife to another man—the basic wrongdoing which not only works against him but which

2. The term is Holloway's.

3. That *The Mayor of Casterbridge* is at least one hundred pages too long has been noted ·by many critics; the unnecessary overabundance of these "suspended moments" testifies to the validity of that criticism.

4. Sigmund Freud, *The Interpretation of Dreams*, 5: 613.

many of his later actions parallel astonishingly—makes possible an extraordinary period of self-discipline." [5] Thus, "he had [been able to use] his one talent of energy to create a position of affluence out of absolutely nothing" (p. 254). Similarly, Henchard's symptomatic outbursts, first evidenced by the sale of his wife, occur when life becomes too difficult for him to control by the efforts of his will alone. His "downfall is essentially the product of his own emotional and moral nature." [6]

It would seem, then, that the possibility of tragedy in the conventional sense, the tragic figure's choosing and taking responsibility for his actions, is precluded. Yet Hardy reads "Plot, or Tragedy" as "the gradual closing in of a situation that comes of ordinary human passions," where even the ability to choose is foreclosed as a possibility, given the internal dialectic of character itself; his view of tragedy lies, instead, in his implied view of consciousness. In addition to the remorse that comes from the realization of actual deeds, the wish, too, becomes the deed in terms of the reality of recognition. Henchard is unable, finally, to carry out his destructive wishes; in his realization of that inability, he turns those urges upon himself. The Greek stage is transformed into the arena of consciousness, that twilight region in which gradations of vision and blindness alternate in each suspended moment. The imagery of light and darkness, and especially of twilight sequences that bear clear resemblances to the descriptions of Egdon Heath, directs our awareness of the movement of Henchard's consciousness within the narrative. While at first his realizations occur after his actions, he later comes to perceive desires in himself that he cannot act upon. Hardy's recasting of ancient tragedy lies in the fact that the protagonist recognizes his responsibility for his own destiny, not by seeing himself as a victim of external fate, but by viewing his consciousness as an instrument of his unknown, unconscious self.

5. See Heilman's introduction to *The Mayor of Casterbridge* (Boston: Riverside, 1962), p. v.

6. Heilman, pp. v-vi.

This universe is defined as early as the scene following Henchard's sale of his wife. While at first there are signs that man's alienation from nature is a fact inherent in the state of things, we come to see a ground level where man and nature are one. Still, it is the *consciousness* of a present alienation that will be the final and distinctly *modern* tragic realization, because is reveals man as "self-alienated" (p. 380). The dynamics of that problem are to be the subject of *Tess* and *Jude*. Note, too, that the following scene occurs exactly at twilight:

> He rose and walked to the entrance with the careful tread of one conscious of his alcoholic load. Some others followed, and they stood looking into the twilight. The difference between the peacefulness of inferior nature and the wilful hostilities of mankind was very apparent at this place. In contrast with the harshness of the act just ended within the tent was the sight of several horses crossing their necks and rubbing each other lovingly as they waited in patience to be harnessed for the homeward journey. Outside the fair, in the valleys and woods, all was quiet. The sun had recently set, and the west heaven was hung with rosy cloud, which seemed permanent, yet slowly changed. To watch it was like looking at some grand feat of stagery from a darkened auditorium. In presence of this scene after the other there was a natural instinct to abjure man as the blot on an otherwise kindly universe; till it was remembered that all terrestrial conditions were intermittent, and that mankind might some night be innocently sleeping when these quiet objects were raging loud. [p. 13]

Henchard has immediately resolved that his crime "was of his own making, and he ought to bear it" (p. 17). When his wife and Elizabeth-Jane enter Casterbridge in search of him nearly twenty years later, they feel that, "recent as [the time] was, [Casterbridge seemed] untouched by the faintest sprinkle of modernism" (p. 30). But this is apparently the same judgment passed on Egdon Heath in *The Return*, before its "inner defect" was laid bare through the dynamics of the characters' consciousness ("The poetry of a scene varies with the minds of the perceivers"). Mother and daughter happen, also, to approach the town at the hour of twilight; yet the "dense trees . . . rendered the road dark as a tunnel, though the open land on each side was still under a faint daylight; in other words, they passed down a midnight between two gloamings" (p. 31). The "pillar" of this community "untouched by . . . modernism" is Michael Henchard—the shock to Susan and Elizabeth-Jane that he is now mayor of the town immediately suggests a possible defect in the present order because of the person who symbolizes it.

Had not Donald Farfrae's "advent coincided with the discussion on corn and bread" outside the King's Arms Hotel, "this history [would have] never been enacted" (p. 42). Henchard's characteristic "oppressive generosity" (p. 37) toward the Scotsman is not unlike the love "to oppressiveness" between Clym and Eustacia.[7] The logic of the relationship between Henchard and Farfrae is similar, if not in many respects identical, to that between the lovers in *The Return*. The inhabitants of Casterbridge begin to view the newly arrived Scot "through a golden haze": "he was to them like the poet of a new school who takes his contemporaries by storm; who is not really new, but is the first to articulate what all his listeners have felt, though but dumbly till then" (p. 61). He plays Stephen Smith to Henchard's Henry Knight, the concept of Clym, (caricatured as propagandist in his parallel to Farfrae, see *The Return*, p. 204) to the drama of Eustacia. Farfrae is "of the age" like Stephen—the scientific, advanced businessman, the material representative of a new order that destroys the symbol of the old, Henchard. But Henchard is also Eustacia on the heath—with the difference that he will respond to his own inner defect and will gradually recognize "the cen-

7. The problem of sex itself does not fully arise until *Tess, Jude*, and to some extent *The Woodlanders*. The similarity between the strong affection of Henchard for Farfrae and the love of Clym and Eustacia is borne out by the many parallels between the pairs.

tral valley" in himself. The realization that occurs in a social metaphor through his combat with Farfrae is but one
version of his tragic awareness to come. Henchard asks Farfrae to stay in Casterbridge less for business reasons than
because he is "so lonely" (p. 64, one of at least three times
he makes the statement) and finds a friend in the Scot. His
"tigerish affection" (p. 104) for Farfrae, like his late, dependent love for Elizabeth-Jane, is really an expression of
that same energy betrayed in his moments of fury. The nature of this energy is fully described later, after his unknowingly false revelation to the girl that she is his daughter:

> He was the kind of man to whom some human object
> for pouring out his heat upon—were it emotive or
> were it choleric—was almost a necessity. The craving
> of his heart for the re-establishment of this tenderest
> human tie had been great during his wife's lifetime,
> and now he had submitted to its mastery without re-
> luctance and without fear. [p. 142]

The "strange warring" that existed in Eustacia's mind has
become central in Henchard now that Hardy has conquered
his past desire to retreat from such a character. The mayor's
feeling for Farfrae is "half-admiring, and yet . . . was not
without a dash of pity for the tastes of any one who could
care to give his mind to such finnikin details" (p. 87) of
business matters. He is compelled to confess his mind, including the two great secrets of his past, to the one man he
can consider a friend; Farfrae's response, of course, is in-
dicative of their differences:

> ". . . I sank into one of those gloomy fits I sometimes
> suffer from, on account of the loneliness of my domes-
> tic life, when the world seems to have the blackness of
> hell, and, like Job, I curse the day that gave me birth."
> "Ah, now, I never feel like it," said Farfrae. [p. 90]

The contraries of Henchard's nature begin to emerge; they
are not so much the contraries of Hardy's own imagination
that we have seen in the juxtaposition of the mayor and

Farfrae, Clym and Eustacia, or Smith and Knight. Rather, he is the product of Hardy's full investigation, at long last, of the darkest and most determining layer of the psyche. His "ambiguous gaze" seems at one moment "to mean satisfaction, and at another fiery disdain" (p. 97). He seeks to punish himself for the past in his dutiful love and care for Susan and Elizabeth-Jane ("to castigate himself with the thorns which these restitutory acts brought in their train," p. 95). Here, his acts stem directly from his conscious intentions because his design is within the control of his willful energy: "He was as kind to her [Susan] as a man, mayor, and churchwarden [all his roles in harmony in this realm] could possibly be" (p. 99).

Henchard's amazement that things are working out well, however, is accompanied by trepidation. Twilight begins in this symbolic statement of the relationship between Henchard and Farfrae:

> Friendship between man and man; what a rugged strength there was in it, as evinced by these two. And yet the seed that was to lift the foundation of this friendship was at that moment taking root in a chink of its structure. [p. 110]

The fateful logic of Henchard's character pervades the world of the novel. Abel Whittle, who returns at the end of the book, tries to explain to Farfrae that his being late for work is beyond his control ("Ye see it can't be helped," p. 113), just as Henchard himself described the supposed impossibility of turning bad wheat into wholesome wheat by declaring "it can't be done" (p. 41; the ramifications of even these incidents reveal the incredibly complex and interrelated aspects of every level of the book). When Farfrae criticizes Henchard for his outrageous treatment of Abel, he is "bitterly hurt" (p. 114). It is on the level of his needs that Henchard responds most deeply, for it is there that the true drama takes place. He now regrets having told his secrets to the Scotsman and begins to think of him with "a dim dread" (p. 116): once the giver feels rejected, the energy first directed as affection (really "emotive") is transformed into its opposite, a burgeoning hostility ("choleric"). The translation of Clym's loves into hates that described Eustacia is not inapplicable here; the settings are similar too—the backdrop for Henchard is his own threatening mind; for Eustacia, the heath. Just as Henchard did penance for his first crime through an energy that created affluence out of nothing, he is "courteous—too courteous" to Farfrae after the Whittle incident, thus displaying a "good breeding which now for the first time showed itself among the qualities of a man he had hitherto thought undisciplined" (p. 117). When inner circumstances permit, Henchard is in full control. But the flaw exists within the very structure of the foundation; twilight comes slowly, but with a relentless inner logic.

Henchard's firing of Farfrae is determined by an internal impulse that acts upon him, and thus differs from those events he has been able to fashion to his liking through conscious energy. His remorseful awareness that his action is irreversible foreshadows the events to come:

> Henchard went home, apparently satisfied. But in the morning, when his jealous temper had passed away, his heart sank within him at what he had said and done. He was the more disturbed when he found that this time Farfrae was determined to take him at his word. [p. 124]

Hardy soon describes the underlayer of unconscious consistency that has occasioned the breach:

> Those tones showed that, though under a long reign of self-control he had become Mayor and churchwarden and what not, there was still the same unruly volcanic stuff beneath the rind of Michael Henchard as when he had sold his wife at Weydon Fair. [p. 129]

When Farfrae establishes his own business, the two become outright competitors, which was the secret desire of Henchard's "volcanic" core. Our growing awareness of the decrees of the interior allows the artist to introduce the definitive statement cited at the beginning of the chapter:

> Character is Fate, said Novalis, and Farfrae's character was just the reverse of Henchard's, who might not inaptly be described as Faust has been described—as a vehement gloomy being who had quitted the ways of vulgar men without light to guide him on a better way. [p. 131]

The consequence of Henchard's uncontrolled action is the narrative recognition of tragedy as Hardy conceives it. Immediately following the pronouncement, Henchard receives a letter from Lucetta and his fall becomes imminent. Again, the quality of Henchard's character permeates the fictional world: we are told, for example, of Elizabeth-Jane's "chaos called consciousness" (pp. 135–36) as she cares for her dying mother.

That the logic of the plot is a dramatization of the logic of Henchard's character becomes clear. His loneliness is now mirrored in the world of fact about him: "Henchard's wife was dissevered from him by death; his friend and helper Farfrae by estrangement; Elizabeth-Jane by ignorance" (p. 139). The next blow occurs when he illicitly reads Susan's note disclosing Elizabeth-Jane's true parentage: he "regarded the paper as if it were a window-pane through which he saw for miles" (p. 143). And he begins, too, to accept responsibility rather than to rely upon his usual moody attitude, " 'I am to suffer, I perceive' ": "through his passionate head there stormed this thought— that the blasting disclosure was what he had deserved" (pp. 143–44). But his "headstrong faculties" (p. 130) continue to dominate his conscious perception, while the artist reminds us again of the true nature of things:

> Misery taught him nothing more than defiant endurance of it. His wife was dead, and the first impulse for revenge died with the thought that she was beyond him. He looked out at the night as at a fiend. Hen-

chard, like all his kind, was superstitious, and he could not help thinking that the concatenation of events this evening had produced was the scheme of some sinister intelligence bent on punishing him. *Yet they had developed naturally.* If he had not revealed his past history to Elizabeth he would not have searched the drawer for papers, and so on. [p. 144; my italics]

The narrative trajectory moves from the artist's revelation of Henchard's character to Henchard's own recognition of facts in the external sphere that reflect his still unknown inner nature. As the world of events closes upon him, he enters a tragic universe of his own making. As twilight begins, the landscape reflects his mood; yet his perception remains partial, as the tragic universe still lacks one element, the protagonist's recognition of his own position:

Above the cliff, and behind the river, rose a pile of buildings, and in front of the pile a square mass cut into the sky. It was like a pedestal lacking a statue. This missing figure, without which the design remained incomplete, was, in truth, the corpse of a man; for the square mass formed the base of the gallows, the extensive buildings at the back being the county gaol.

Another feature of the full tragedy to come, recognition by the community, is suggested, too, as the passage continues:

In the meadow where Henchard now walked the mob were wont to gather whenever an execution took place, and there to the tune of the roaring weir they stood and watched the spectacle.

The exaggeration which darkness imparted to the glooms of this region impressed Henchard more than he had expected. The lugubrious harmony of the spot with his domestic situation was too perfect for him, impatient of effects, scenes, and adumbrations. It reduced his heartburning to melancholy, and he exclaimed, "Why the deuce did I come here!"

Then, the invocation of the suspended moment, as the fires
die out and the gloom sets in:

> He was like one who had half fainted, and could nei-
> ther recover nor complete the swoon. In words he
> could blame his wife, but not in his heart; and had he
> obeyed the wise directions outside her letter this pain
> would have been spared him for long—possibly for
> ever. [pp. 145–46]

But to be "spared . . . for ever" by one less act is, of
course, an impossibility in this universe. "The return of
the repressed" has many pathways by which it may reach
Henchard's consciousness; in this case, Newson's inevitable
return is the result of an act of twenty years past, despite
the mayor's present remorse.

The consequences of Farfrae's dismissal have shown that
act to be of the "same unruly volcanic stuff" as Henchard's
original crime of selling his wife. It is as though the results
of the first act twenty years before remain latent while the
ramifications of his second irreversible action take their
toll. "His bitter disappointment at finding Elizabeth-Jane
to be none of his, and himself a childless man, had left
an emotional void in Henchard which he unconsciously
craved to fill" (p. 169). Lucetta's return seems to provide
him again with the opportunity he lost in the consequences
of firing Farfrae, but he loses her to his former friend as
well.

Farfrae's prosperity as a merchant in his own right signifies the advent of the new order in its material form, the
result of the decline of the old community as embodied in
Henchard's fall. "The character of the town's trading had
changed from bulk to multiplicity" (p. 195), indicating an
ominous fragmentation of the bonds of society. The original agricultural community in the novel was altruistic
rather than competitive, where even "over-clothes [in the
market-place] were worn as if they were an inconvenience,
a hampering necessity" (p. 175). But the "multiplicity" of

the new commercial order, symbolized, too, in Farfrae's introduction of a new agricultural machine (pp. 191–92), is a sign of the surfacing of an inner defect. The changes wrought in the harmonious, almost noncompetitive, old order emerge in a description of Farfrae's revealing his own self-alienation. However, because he encounters no setback in terms of the mediocre demands of his own nature (remember Henchard's "dash of pity" for him earlier), he remains unconscious of his inner fragmentation as well as of the one without: "the curious double strands in Farfrae's thread of life—the commercial and the romantic—were very distinct at times. Like the colors in a variegated cord, those contrasts could be seen intertwisted, yet not mingling" (p. 183).

Consciousness of the inadequacy of the old order is "modern" consciousness; but the facts of the transition from old to new are material changes—externalizations of the inner defect which impress none but those characters capable of tragic possibilities. The bonfires on the heath have symbolized the fact that community is a matter of interdependence; for example:

> Nearly the whole town had gone into the fields. The Casterbridge populace still retained the primitive habit of helping one another in time of need; and thus, though the corn belonged to the farming section of the little community—that inhabiting the Durnover quarter—the remainder was no less interested in the labor of getting it home. [p. 223]

When the fires change from group centers to multitudes of individual locations (from "bulk" to "multiplicity"), collective altruism (which we see now not as altruism at all, but as a dependent love whose real roots come to light in the disclosure of Henchard's volcanic layers) becomes a vicious, egoistic struggle among divided men, fragmented as a society and fragmented within themselves. A true dialectic of need was operative in the old community:

The farmer's income was ruled by the wheat-crop within his own horizon, and the wheat-crop by the weather. Thus, in person, he became a sort of flesh-barometer, with feelers always directed to the sky and wind around him. The local atmosphere was everything to him; the atmosphere of other countries a matter of indifference. The people, too, who were not farmers, the rural multitude, saw in the god of the weather a more important personage than they do now. Indeed, the feeling of the peasantry in this matter was so intense as to be almost unrealizable in these equable days. Their impulse was well-nigh to prostrate themselves in lamentation before untimely rains and tempests, which came as the Alastor of those households whose crime it was to be poor. [pp. 211–12]

But the flaw in the structure, if not recognizable already, may become apparent—an ostensible altruism, is, in reality, an expression of egoistic concerns: "The townsfolk understood every fluctuation in the rustic's condition, for it affected their receipts as much as the laborer's" (p. 70). Thus, we see the irony of the "Royal Personage" passing through Casterbridge on his way "to inaugurate an immense engineering work out that way" (p. 302): the highest representative of the old order is engaged in the "zealous promotion of designs for placing the art of farming on a more scientific footing" (p. 302). The inner defect works from within the contradictions of its old shell to transform itself dialectically into the new order, whose self-immolation is laid bare.

The modern tragic figure, of course, finally recognizes the falseness of any fires, whether collective illusions or fragmented, egocentric palliatives. The struggle between Henchard and Farfrae "constitutes the narrative and the unity of the book, and. . . predominantly defines its significance." [8] Yet the struggle becomes Henchard's struggle with himself—Farfrae is the externalization of the mayor's, and

8. Holloway, *The Charted Mirror*, p. 103.

the community's, inner defect, its "central valley." Once it enters the realm of consciousness, it shows itself to be the same "hitherto unrecognized original" of which we had glimpses in *The Return of the Native,* and which is now revealed in a concentrated vision. The Scotsman functions in a manner which externalizes the development of Henchard's own contradictions. The mayor's gradual awareness of his inner self is the organizational and perceptive center of the novel. The prophet Fall's remark to Henchard lends traditional mythic significance to this distinctly modern tragedy: " 'Twill be more like living in Revelations this autumn than in England" (p. 215). The November aspect of Egdon Heath broods behind the entire narrative.

Event upon event builds up the dramatization of "the momentum of his character [which] knew no patience. At this turn of the scales [Henchard's financial ruin] he remained silent" (p. 219). The artist emphasizes the difference between his perception of events and that of the still unconscious Henchard: "The movements of his mind seemed to tend to the thought that some power was working against him" (p. 219). With the inevitable return of the repressed original crime in public, the furmity-woman's indictment of Henchard the judge, both past and present begin to enfold him:

> Small as the police-court incident had been in itself, it formed the edge or turn in the incline of Henchard's fortunes. On that day—almost at that minute—he passed the ridge of prosperity and honor, and began to descend rapidly on the other side. It was strange how soon he sank in esteem. Socially he had received a startling fillip downwards; and, having already lost commercial buoyancy from rash transactions, the velocity of his descent in both aspects became accelerated every hour. [p. 251]

Thus the tragedy, before recognition by the protagonist, displays a dual aspect: the personal and the historical, the private and the public. A discrepancy now exists between

Henchard's individual life and his public identity, roles which were apparently in harmony when his drive alone was able to control his actions. The narrative begins to recognize the hitherto undiscovered original in the identity of Henchard's deepest impulses and the latent egoism of the ostensibly altruistic traditional community. The case is not unlike the one described by Conrad in *The Nigger of the Narcissus,* when he reveals the true bonds of the crew's community in relation to Wait: "The latent egoism of tenderness to suffering appeared in the developing anxiety not to see him die." [9] In *The Mayor,* landscape again takes on symbolic twilight significance: "The low land grew blacker, and the sky a deeper grey" (p. 260).

While, for a moment, the possibility of equilibrium appears in Henchard's working for Farfrae, it is as deceptive as Clym's supposed reharmonization with the heath in his furze-cutting. Both are aborted by the force of a necessary "mutually destructive interdependence": for Clym, Eustacia; for Henchard, his deeper self. Even the parallel of Clym's blindness with Farfrae's unconsciousness becomes clear: "Henchard, a poor man in [Farfrae's] employ, was not to Farfrae's view the Henchard who had ruled him. Yet he was not only the same man, but that man with his sinister qualities, formerly latent, quickened into life by his buffetings" (p. 276). The full concentration of the tragedy occurs within Henchard's sphere alone: the entire world of the novel is but an external counterpart, a mirror, to the organizing perception of his mind. While he suggests he may act out his wishes by declaring that, if he meets Farfrae, "I won't answer for my deeds!" (p. 270),

> . . . again he stopped short. The truth was that, as may be divined, he had quite intended to effect a grand catastrophe at the end of this drama [of his reading to Farfrae Lucetta's early love letters to himself] by reading out the name; he had come to the house with

9. Joseph Conrad, *The Nigger of the Narcissus* (New York, 1926), p. 138.

no other thought. But sitting here in cold blood he could not do it. Such a wrecking of hearts appalled even him. His quality was such that he could have annihilated them both in the heat of action; but to accomplish the deed by oral poison was beyond the nerve of his enmity. [p. 284]

In fact, later, "Henchard had been as good as his word" (p. 292) in his promise to restore the letters to Lucetta. Henchard's conscious acts, when they prove devastating, are the work of inner powers beyond the control of his willful drive. And, almost as proof of his intention to be responsible to others, the damage that results from actions beyond his conscious control is pain to himself alone. Again, the laws of Henchard's nature work in the book as a whole: in the incident of the love letters, "though [Lucetta's] had been rather the laxity of inadvertence than of intention, that episode, if known, was not the less likely to operate fatally between herself and her husband [Farfrae]" (p. 301); in the form of a public act, too, the skimmington (paralleling in preparation and occurrence the arrival of the royal visitor).

After a physical struggle with Farfrae—supposedly to the death—the contradictions in Henchard's nature are glaring, as he crouches in "self-reproach" (p. 316) on the sacks in the barn: "Its womanliness sat tragically on the figure of so stern a piece of virility" (p. 316). At still another moment of possible equilibrium, when Henchard has reestablished affectionate ties with Elizabeth-Jane, Newson's appearance seems to set things off once more. But Henchard, of course, responds from the "volcanic" layer by misinforming the sailor that his daughter is dead. Even as soon as the mariner leaves, he knows that his new sin will come back to destroy him. The fact of recrimination becomes less and less necessary for the true nature of the process to be revealed: "Then Henchard, scarcely believing the evidence of his senses, rose from his seat amazed at what he had done. It had been the

impulse of a moment" (p. 338), as "his jealous soul" vi-
ciously "[buries] his grief in his own heart" (p. 339).

Twilight has become night: "The whole land ahead of
him was as darkness itself" (p. 341); there must he wander
now that his deepest nature, in conflict with his one-sided
conscious desires, has extinguished all light. The appearance of his own reflection in the river he intends to be his
grave is an external statement of the self-recognition to
come. His egoism, his love, and his hate battle within, as
there "came to the surface that idiosyncrasy of [his] which
had ruled his courses from the beginning and had mainly
made him what he was. . . . Time had been when such
instinctive opposition [to the marriage of Elizabeth-Jane
and Farfrae] would have taken shape in action. But he was
not now the Henchard of former days" (pp. 350–51).

Henchard is finally becoming aware of his dual nature,
and Hardy assigns to the recognition the qualities of uni-
versality, in his conceptual prelude:

> There is an outer chamber of the brain in which
> thoughts unowned, unsolicited, and of noxious kind,
> are sometimes allowed to wander for a moment prior
> to being sent off whence they came. One of these
> thoughts sailed into Henchard's ken now. . . . [He]
> shuddered, and exclaimed, "God forbid such a thing!
> Why should I still be subject to these visitations of the
> devil when I try so hard to keep him away?" [p. 354]

Here lies the core of Henchard's nature: it defines man's
area of responsibility within this universe. Tragedy consists
of the consciousness of these limitations and man's ability
to make his way through its chaotic darkness, the fate dictated by his own unconscious. "I—Cain—go alone as I deserve—an outcast and a vagabond. But my punishment is
not greater than I can bear" (p. 361). Yet the prospect of
death also intrudes upon Henchard's mind: "Part of his
wish to wash his hands of life arose from his perception of
its contrarious inconsistencies—of Nature's jaunty readiness

to support unorthodox social principles" (p. 368). Elizabeth-Jane's burial of the dead bird that was Henchard's "hitherto undiscovered" wedding-gift occasions further symbolic statement: "She went out, looked at the cage, buried the starved little singer, and from that hour her heart softened towards the self-alienated man" (p. 380).

Henchard's modern tragic stance is his final recognition that he is trapped within the prison of his ego, subject to the unknown forces of unconscious instinctual underpinnings whose inconsistencies are mirrored in an equally dark and unknown external nature. But Hardy does not imply that this condition is in itself a law of existence. The cell of the self is the result of a process within history, a dialectic of man and nature in the form of society. We have seen that Henchard is representative of a broader process: the dynamics of his nature are reflected in the movement of the community he once symbolized.

With the establishment of his notion of "modern" consciousness, Hardy will move to an examination of the workings of those processes themselves. *The Mayor of Casterbridge* is a study, finally, in the discovery of self-alienation. It was necessary to emphasize the social processes involved in that discovery because the recognition itself is the product of an inescapable dialectic of community—a dialectic between man and nature. "Nature's jaunty readiness to support unorthodox social principles," given the revelation of Henchard's inner self, suggested a host of problems to be investigated, a new direction issuing from past and present discoveries.

5 The Woodlanders

While he was writing *The Woodlanders* in 1886, Hardy noted on March 4: "Novel-writing as an art cannot go backward. Having reached the analytic stage it must transcend it by going still further in the same direction" (*Life,* p. 177). While the ultimate drift of his statement found expression to his own satisfaction in *The Dynasts,* the nature of his thoughts about the direction prose fiction should take anticipates the atmosphere of his last three great novels—a world that sprung directly from the almost "analytic" breakthrough of *The Mayor of Casterbridge.* While the old sensibilities remain, these last novels seem to have been composed with a freedom lacking in his previous books—from the rich, even low-keyed, woodlands, through the wanderings of Tess, and finally, to the stark and austere portraits of Jude and Sue Bridehead.

Marty South's emergence from her father's woodland cottage into the night is described with imagery we have traced from *The Return of the Native* through *The Mayor of Casterbridge;* a change, however, has taken place because of the absence of a twilight sensibility: "For her eyes were fresh from the blaze, and here there was no street lamp or lantern to form a kindly transition between the inner glare and the outer dark" (p. 15). The lines are drawn more firmly as Hardy sets out beyond *The Mayor of Casterbridge.* The community sensibility is presented with a new richness: while the old order has grown progressively weaker in the development of the novels, its character, perhaps for that reason, has never been presented so forcefully. The clarity of the rural portraits of Giles Winterbourne and Marty South stands in sharp contrast to Hardy's portrayal of the decadence of the intrusive urban influences, Fitzpiers and Felice Charmond. Grace Melbury and her father, torn between the great contraries, attempt to mediate between the extremes. And yet it is the smooth, low-keyed fullness of *The Woodlanders* that sets it apart from the almost oppressive emotion and heartsickness of *Tess* and *Jude;* in its premises, however, it is the natural prelude to both those haunting works.

In *The Mayor,* Hardy briefly uses two similies, both of which recur early in this novel. In one confrontation with Elizabeth-Jane, Henchard is seen "moving like a great tree in a wind" (*Mayor,* p. 141); when he reads of her true parentage, he "regarded the paper as if it were a window-pane through which he saw for miles" (*Mayor,* p. 143). Just as Henchard and all he represents have fallen by dint of the revelation of a translatable inner defect, a great swaying tree symbolizes the strength of Marty's father. A peculiar obsession, alien to his public character, urges him to order the tree cut down; the operation results in his death.[1] And as the paper on which Susan's note is written becomes a windowpane, so Hardy pursues the metaphor as he suggests modes of consciousness in *The Woodlanders:*

> Looking at the van from the back the spectator could thus see, through its interior, a square piece of the same sky and landscape that he saw without, but intruded on by the profiles of the seated passengers, who, as they rumbled onward, their lips moving and heads nodding in animated private converse, remained in cheerful unconsciousness that their mannerisms and facial peculiarities were sharply defined to the public eye. [pp. 3–4]

In the opening pages of the novel, Hardy immediately distinguishes between the consciousness of loneliness and that of solitude; the former is a distinctively social alienation, the latter, a natural harmony. The context of each kind of consciousness is made perceptible through the landscape:

> The physiognomy of a deserted highway expresses solitude to a degree that is not reached by mere dales or

1. Holloway, *The Charted Mirror,* p. 101.

downs, and bespeaks a tomb-like stillness more em-
phatic than that of glades and pools. The contrast of
what is with what might be, probably accounts for this.
To step, for instance, at the place under notice, from
the edge of the plantation into the adjoining thoroughfare, and pause amid its emptiness for a moment, was
to exchange by the act of a single stride the simple absence of human companionship for an incubus of the
forlorn. [p. 1]

The real is at the same time the symbolic, as we shall see
so clearly in *Tess*.

There is an almost bitter cynicism in the fact that the
foppish barber is the first character to appear in this woodland setting—a comment on the castration and rape of the
rural community (the cutting down of John South's tree
and Marty's loss of her hair) by inherently impotent, while
circumstantially powerful, forces. (These include self-
destructive impulses as exemplified in old South, and a
material, or commercial, fragmentation resulting in self-
alienation as embodied in Marty's sale of her hair.)

Hardy's diary entry for March 28, 1888, includes his direct statement about the implications of individual isolation, of the alienating self-consciousness played out progressively in the novels since *The Mayor*: "Each individual is
conscious of *himself*, but nobody conscious of themselves
collectively" (*Life*, pp. 206–07). While Hardy recorded the
note in connection with his observations of London life,
this erstwhile urban consciousness is now at the heart of
the rural world: "Her own existence, and not Mr. Melbury's, was the centre of Marty's consciousness, and it was
in relation to this that the matter [Melbury's intention for
Giles to have his daughter] struck her as she slowly withdrew" (p. 19). Indeed, it is this perception on Marty's part
that furnishes her with the decision to sell her hair. Self-
consciousness works, then, in the rural order's undermining
of its own strength. But the integrity of the community remains if its strength does not:

> Hardly anything could be more isolated or more self-contained than the lives of these two [Giles and Marty] walking here in the lonely hour before day, when grey shades, material and mental, are so very grey. And yet their lonely courses formed no detached design at all, but were part of the pattern in the great web of human doings then weaving in both hemispheres from the White Sea to Cape Horn. [p. 21]

Even though the flaw in the structure of the rural world is now constantly apparent, Giles's and Marty's adherence to renunciation (she, "doomed to sacrifice desire to obligation," p. 174), a selflessness that issues from a belief in the forms of community, sets them apart from the egoistic self-indulgence of Fitzpiers and Mrs. Charmond. The nature of the doctor's intellectual pursuits are nearly a comic commentary on the only apparent reflection between his studies and the narrative action: " 'Here am I,' he said, 'endeavouring to carry on simultaneously the study of physiology and transcendental philosophy, the material world and the ideal, so as to discover if possible a point of contact between them; and your finer sense is quite offended!' " (p. 156). While Fitzpiers allows impulse to rule his judgment, Grace forces reason to rule desire. But opposed to the mental machinations of both Fitzpiers and Grace, as well as of Mrs. Charmond, Giles and Marty know only a single method that must endure no matter the consequences. While both communal figures stand aside, brokenhearted at their respective fates (and while, if they had not a common purpose apart from their personal emotions, they would be embittered toward one another), Mrs. Charmond, like Fitzpiers, constantly indulges in self-parodies similar to the doctor's incongruous Romantic musings: " 'O! why were we given hungry hearts and wild desires if we have to live in a world like this?' " (p. 237).

Grace, bound to Fitzpiers by law, is an index of the contrasting sensibilities nurtured by the values she calls upon to force judgment upon her impulses; similarly, her father revolts against his conscience in favor of his social judgment. Once her husband leaves her, her mind is freed to meet her own desires again in Giles:

> He looked and smelt like Autumn's very brother, his face being sunburnt to wheat-colour, his eyes blue as corn-flowers, his sleeves and leggins dyed with fruit-stains, his hands clammy with the sweet juice of apples, his hat sprinkled with pips, and everywhere about him that atmosphere of cider which at its first return each season has such an indescribable fascination for those who have been born and bred among orchards. Her heart rose from its late sadness like a released bough; her senses revelled in the sudden lapse back to Nature unadorned. The consciousness of having to be genteel because of her husband's profession, the veneer of artificiality which she had acquired at the fashionable schools, were thrown off, and she became the crude country girl of her latent early instincts.
>
> Nature was bountiful, she thought. No sooner had she been cast aside by Edred Fitzpiers than another being, impersonating chivalrous and undiluted manliness, had arisen out of the earth ready to her hand. This, however, was an excursion of the imagination which she did not wish to encourage. . . .
>
> Her abandonment to the seductive hour and scene after her sense of ill-usage, her revolt for the nonce against social law, her passionate desire for primitive life may have showed in her face. [pp. 246–48]

Nature, in the form of the community order, becomes the ground scale against which Hardy's protagonists weigh their lives. But their tragedies lie in the fact that they become conscious of the meaning and value of the earth only because of their present separation from it. Hardy clearly addresses himself to a Romantic problem:

> Man has "fallen," not so much into sin as into the original sin of self-consciousness, into his present sub-

ject-object relation to nature, where because his consciousness is what separates him from nature, the primary conscious feeling is one of separation.[2]

Even Marty and Giles, of course, are the victims of self-consciousness; but, because they can still adhere to the crumbling old order (because it is still real to their perceptions) and its intended aims of community, they are barred from the status of tragic figures within the modern context. A few years before *The Woodlanders* (probably during the composition of *The Mayor*), Hardy had written: "All are caged birds; the only difference lies in the size of the cage" (*Life*, p. 171, May 28, 1885).

Grace recognizes her true affinities only after the reality of marriage. Her father, too, suffers in its wake:

> He had entirely lost faith in his own judgment. That judgment on which he had relied for so many years seemed recently like a false companion unmasked to have disclosed unexpected depths of hypocrisy and speciousness, where all had seemed solidity. He felt almost afraid to form a conjecture on the weather, or the time, or the fruit-promise, so great was his self-mistrust. [p. 270]

The window imagery that recurs throughout the novel emphasizes again the full force of Hardy's early remark, "a scene varies with the minds of the perceivers," as the sin of self-consciousness, and, by implication, its social origins, loom ever larger. Once more, Melbury:

> The scene to him was not the material environment of his person, but a tragic vision that travelled with him like an envelope. Through this vision the incidents of the moment but gleamed confusedly here and there, as an outer landscape through the high-coloured scenes of a stained window. [p. 277]

As the outlines of the last two novels become apparent, Grace and Giles for a moment resemble Sue Bridehead and

2. Northrop Frye, *A Study of English Romanticism*, pp. 17–18.

Jude, as they discuss the divorce laws: "To hear these two Arcadian innocents talk of imperial law would have made a humane person weep who should have known what a dangerous structure they were building up on their supposed knowledge. They remained in thought, like children in the presence of the incomprehensible" (p. 340). The meaning of Hardy's remark early in the novel now achieves completion: "dramas of a grandeur and unity truly Sophoclean are enacted in the real, by virtue of the concentrated passions and closely-knit interdependence of the lives therein" (pp. 4–5). Grace offers Giles a kiss, ignorant of his knowledge that the divorce is impossible:

> For the last several minutes he had seen this great temptation approaching him in regular siege; and now it had come. The wrong, the social sin, of now taking advantage of the offer of her lips, had a magnitude in the eyes of one whose life had been so primitive, so ruled by household laws as Giles's, which can hardly be explained. [p. 350]

Winterbourne's integrity lies in his adherence to "household laws," as direct a reference as any in Hardy to similar Aristotelian laws of community whose transgression constitutes a "social sin." [3] Grace's position is similar in structure to Antigone's, but because the context is a modern one, she is subject to no illusions whatsoever about the community. She is an "impressionable creature, who combined modern nerves with primitive feelings, and was doomed by such co-existence to be numbered among the distressed" (p. 358). Seeking an identity in nature, she sees through social laws

3. *Antigone* affords a good example of a classical comparison. Although Antigone comes up against the force of the *polis* instead of modern individualism, the structure of the tragedy is practically identical. The laws of the past are upheld by the true members of the household community; Antigone's duty is to bury her brother in defiance of the coming wave of new laws embodied in the *polis*. In Hardy's *Jude*, the *attempted* new order will be the "experiment." For a full discussion of Hardy and the classics, see Rutland, *Thomas Hardy*, pp. 20–45.

that really violate what is natural; Giles, on the other hand, is denied such a vision. Because Grace is a refugee fleeing from the dying world, she is at one moment ready to experiment like Jude and Sue. Realizing her selfishness, late in the novel she calls Giles to come in from the rain: " 'Come to me, dearest! I don't mind what they say or what they think of us any more!' " (p. 374; Hardy's italics).

With Giles's death and the repentant return of Grace's husband, the novel stops short of the direction Hardy will take in his last two great works. The abiding impression of *The Woodlanders* is that of our last and clearest view of the community sensibility. While in his work up to *The Mayor of Casterbridge* Hardy at least tried to impute an always refreshing permanence to the rural order, we are left here with the knowledge that, with the tenuous reunion of Grace and Fitzpiers, the life-force of the old order has vanished forever. The loss of the regenerative power of the rural sensibility is made clear by the end of the novel. Giles is dead, and "Marty South alone, of all the women in Hintock and the world, had approximated to Winterbourne's level of intelligent intercourse with Nature" (p. 399). She stands by his grave unaccompanied, Grace having departed from the place forever, as Hardy laments the final moments of a passing order:

> As this solitary and silent girl stood there in the moonlight, a straight slim figure, clothed in a plaitless gown, the contours of womanhood so undeveloped as to be scarcely perceptible in her, the marks of poverty and toil effaced by the misty hour, she touched sublimity at points, and looked almost like a being who had rejected with indifference the attribute of sex for the loftier quality of abstract humanism. She stooped down and cleared away the withered flowers that Grace and herself had laid there the previous week, and put her fresh ones in their place.
>
> "Now, my own, own love," she whispered, "you are mine, and only mine; for she has forgot 'ee at last, al-

though for her you died! But I—whenever I get up I'll think of 'ee, and whenever I lie down I'll think of 'ee again. Whenever I plant the young larches I'll think that none can plant as you planted; and whenever I split a gad, and whenever I turn the cider wring, I'll say none could do it like you. If I ever forget your name let me forget home and heaven! . . . But no, no, my love, I never can forget 'ee; for you was a good man, and did good things!" [pp. 443–44]

6 *Tess of the d'Urbervilles*

"That which, socially, is a great tragedy," wrote Hardy on May 5, 1889, "may be in Nature no alarming circumstance" (*Life*, p. 218). It is perhaps best to view *Tess of the d'Urbervilles* from this capsulized perspective. The confrontation within man of his natural and social components, a confrontation that is tragic when recognized self-consciously, is the psychological battleground of Hardy's last, and probably greatest, novels. As man's self-consciousness grows, "the mutually destructive interdependence of spirit and flesh" becomes

> A woeful fact—. . . the human race is too extremely developed for its corporeal conditions, the nerves being evolved to an activity abnormal in such an environment. Even the higher animals are in excess in this respect. It may be questioned if Nature, or what we call Nature, so far back when she crossed the line from invertebrates to vertebrates, did not exceed her mission. This planet does not supply the materials for happiness to higher existences. Other planets may, though one can hardly see now. [*Life*, p. 218, April 7, 1889]

> "Did you say the stars were worlds, Tess?"
> "Yes."
> "All like ours?"
> "I don't know; but I think so. They sometimes seem to be like the apples on our stubbard-tree. Most of them splendid and sound—a few blighted."
> "Which de we live on—a splendid one or a blighted one?"
> "A blighted one."
> " 'Tis very unlucky that we didn't pitch on a sound

one, when there were so many more of 'em!"

"Yes." [pp. 33–34]

Amid the din of bitter moral outrage with which the press and the public initially reacted to *Tess,* Hardy's prefaces to the novel reaffirm the historical aspect of his work. He saw the controversy raised by the book as the whimper of the "too genteel reader, who cannot endure to have said what everybody nowadays thinks and feels" (1891 preface); he also wanted to "repeat that a novel is an impression, not an argument; and there the matter must rest" (1892 preface).

It becomes increasingly clear that Tess, while physically a member of the rural community, is nevertheless alienated from its society. When her father, a vestige of the now-decadent d'Urberville lineage, claims that she is "queer," we may infer a mythical genetic component to her "dreaminess." [1] Tess's mother, on the other hand, who is descended from a long line of thoroughly common folk, believes " 'she's tractable at bottom. Leave her to me' " (p. 29). Thus, at the start of the novel, even though "Tess Durbeyfield at this time of her life was a mere vessel of emotion untinctured by experience" (p. 13), the tensions that will create her tragic posture are already suggested. While folk wisdom and custom seem to require no punishment for her early debauche, she will have to face the prejudices of still firmer social codes in the future, and will respond with rebellion. But even custom, in the additional form of Joan Durbeyfield's advice to her daughter not to confess to Angel, opposes Tess's desires as well.

The quality of her reveries is disclosed as early as the night-ride with her brother. Her abstracted state of mind, including her personal transcendence of her family's vain aspirations, brings on the catastrophe of Prince's death. By making her feel more responsible to her family than ever, the highway accident causes her in turn to seek out the Stoke-d'Urbervilles and, thus, to meet Alec:

1. Holloway, *The Charted Mirror,* p. 98.

Tess fell more deeply into reverie than ever, her back
leaning against the hives. The mute procession past her
shoulders of trees and hedges became attached to fan-
tastic scenes outside reality, and the occasional heave
of the wind became the sigh of some immense sad soul,
conterminous with the universe in space, and with history in time.

Then, examining the mesh of events in her own life,
she seemed to see the vanity of her father's pride; the
gentlemanly suitor awaiting herself in her mother's
fancy; to see him as a grimacing personage, laughing at
her poverty, and her shrouded knightly ancestry.
Everything grew more and more extravagant, and she
no longer knew how time passed. A sudden jerk shook
her in her seat, and Tess awoke from the sleep into
which she, too, had fallen. [pp. 34–35]

And just as her dreaminess brings about her meeting with
Alec, that same quality attracts Angel Clare and causes him
to single her out from the other dairymaids at Talbothays:

Clare looked round upon her, seated with the others.

She was not looking towards him. Indeed, owing to
his long silence, his presence in the room was almost
forgotten.

"I don't know about ghosts," she was saying, "but I
do know that our souls can be made to go outside our
bodies when we are alive."

The dairyman turned to her with his mouth full, his
eyes charged with serious inquiry, and his great knife
and fork (breakfasts were breakfasts here) planted erect
on the table, *like the beginning of a gallows.*

"What—really now? And is it so, maidy?" he said.

"A very easy way to feel 'em go," continued Tess, "is
to lie on the grass at night and look straight up at some
big bright star; and, by fixing your mind upon it, you
will soon find that you are hundreds and hundreds of
miles away from your body, which you don't seem to
want at all." [p. 154, my italics]

At this important moment in the book, Hardy's use of symbolic detail (Dairyman Crick's knife and fork poised "like the beginning of a gallows") points toward the resolution of the novel. Crick voices the disbelieving resistance that the entire social order will assume as the novel develops; just as the subject of Tess's conversation here alludes directly to her talk with her brother about the stars preceding the reverie that had produced the accident.

At the close of Tess's first meeting with d'Urberville, Hardy furnishes one of his conceptual commentaries, which implicitly addresses itself to the question of "the mutually destructive interdependence" of the philosophical and artistic eyes in his narratives, as well as to the tensions between and within his characters. In spite of the usual irritation of the unfolding drama caused by these conceptual asides, the affinity between the following passage from *Tess* and an entry from Hardy's notebook affords us a glimpse of the dynamics of the creating mind. In disclosing the positions of his three alienated protagonists within the social mechanism, he taps a central vein in his thought, as he lays out reasons behind the "impression" recorded as a novel:

In the ill-judged execution of the well-judged plan of things the call seldom produces the comer, the man to love rarely coincides with the hour for loving. . . . We may wonder whether at the acme and summit of the human progress these anachronisms will be corrected by a finer intuition, a closer interaction of the social machinery than that which now jolts us round and along; but such completeness is not to be prophesied, or even conceived as possible. Enough that in the present case, as in millions, it was not the two halves of a perfect whole that confronted each other at the perfect moment; a missing counterpart wandered independently about the earth waiting in crass obtuseness till the late time came. Out of which maladroit delay sprang anxieties, disappointments, shocks, catastrophes, and passing-strange destinies. [pp. 48–49]

May 9 [1881]. After infinite trying to reconcile a scientific view of life with the emotional and spiritual, so that they may not be interdestructive, I come to the following:

"General Principles. Law has produced in man a child who cannot but constantly reproach its parent for doing much and yet not all, and constantly say to such parent that it would have been better never to have begun doing than to have *over*done so indecisively; that is, than to have created so far beyond all apparent first intention (on the emotional side), without mending matters by a second intent and execution, to eliminate the evils of a blunder of overdoing. The emotions have no place in a world of defect, and it is a cruel injustice that they should have developed in it.

"If Law itself had consciousness, how the aspect of its creatures would terrify it, fill it with remorse!" [*Life,* pp. 148–49]

A perception of the FAILURE OF THINGS to be what they are meant to be, lends them, in place of the intended interest, a new and greater interest of an unintended kind. [*Life,* p. 124, January 1, 1879]

Before losing her virginity to Alec, Tess, in spite of the glimmerings of a preexistent alienation, is still considered "[l]ike all the cottagers in Blackmoor Vale, . . . steeped in fancies and prefigurative superstitions" (p. 50). Hardy's interplay of visual perspectives in the scene of Tess's departure from home to live at the d'Urberville estate recalls the pattern of the early novels—a pattern distinct and operative again within the wider and deeper foundations established since *The Return of the Native:*

So the girls and their mother all walked together, a child on each side of Tess, holding her hand, and looking at her meditatively from time to time, as at one who was about to do great things; her mother just behind with the smallest; the group forming a picture of honest beauty flanked by innocence, and backed by simple-souled vanity. . . .

[The perspective switches back and forth from the single figure of Tess leaving the group and meeting Alec's carriage to her view of the family] . . . *The new point of view was infectious* (as the children burst into tears). [pp. 58–60, my italics]

As Tess rides away from home with Alec, the landscape performs a dual function, both actual and symbolic: "Rising still, an immense landscape stretched around them on every side; behind the green valley of her birth, before, a gray country of which she knew nothing except from her first brief visit to Trantridge" (p. 62). But, again, Hardy seems to emphasize that Tess's separation from the community does not result from the birth of her illegitimate child. Indeed, rural society would see fit to overlook the infant's illegitimacy. Ironically, it is a social sin only in the eyes of someone like Angel, who is attracted to Tess because of her dreaminess, almost a reciprocal recognition between the alienated protagonists. Just before the "seduction scene," Alec is granted his opportunity precisely because Tess cannot be a part of the drunken crew walking across the fields at night (where, for the "work-folk," "the spirit of the scene, and of the moonlight, and of Nature, seemed harmoniously to mingle with the spirit of wine," p. 84). At the moment of Tess's undoing, "darkness and silence ruled everywhere around" (p. 90). Offering no explanation but simply an "impression," Hardy concludes the first phase of the novel:

Why it was that upon this beautiful feminine tissue, sensitive as gossamer, and practically blank as snow, as yet, there should have been traced such a coarse pattern as it was doomed to receive; why so often the coarse appropriates the finer thus, the wrong man the woman, the wrong woman the man, many thousand years of analytical philosophy have failed to explain to our sense of order. One may, indeed, admit the possibility of a retribution lurking in the present catastrophe. Doubtless some of Tess d'Urberville's mailed ancestors rollicking home from a fray had dealt the same measure even more ruthlessly towards peasant girls of their time. But though to visit the sins of the fathers upon the children may be a morality good enough for divinities, it is scorned by average human nature; and it therefore does not mend the matter.

As Tess's own people down in those retreats are never tired of saying among each other in their fatalistic way: "It was to be." There lay the pity of it. An immeasurable social chasm was to divide our heroine's personality thereafter from that previous self of hers who stepped from her mother's door to try her fortune at Trantridge poultry-farm. [p. 91]

But Tess's leaving Alec is, in itself, an "eminently modern idea . . . —of a woman's not becoming necessarily the chattel and slave of her seducer," an idea that "impressed Hardy [as] being one of the first glimmers of woman's enfranchisement; and he made use of it in succeeding years in more than one case in his fiction and verse," preeminently in *Tess* (*Life*, p. 157). While the folk wisdom of Joan Durbeyfield may decide, " 'Well, we must make the best of it, I suppose. 'Tis nater, after all, and what do please God!' " (p. 104), the daughter will reject her mother's guidance. "Tess's tragedy turns on a secret revealed, that is, on the substitution in Tess of an individualizing morality for the folk instinct of *anonymity* and *concealment*." [2] She also rejects the views of traditional religion and social ethics. Almost every detail in the novel, imagic or descriptive, alludes either to larger symbolic patterns or to future incidents which, in their actuality, also turn on symbolic meanings, according to the dictates of the "naturalistic premise" [3] of the book.

In place of the excitement of her return, and the interest it had inspired, she saw before her a long and

2. Dorothy Van Ghent, *The English Novel*, p. 206.
3. Ibid., p. 204.

stony highway which she had to tread, without aid, and with little sympathy. Her expression was then terrible, and she could have hidden herself in a tomb. [p. 106]

In the recurrence of the twilight metaphor, we see the tension in her present situation alive with Hardyesque tragic possibilities:

The only exercise that Tess took at this time was after dark; and it was then, when out in the woods, that she seemed least solitary. She knew how to hit to a hair's-breadth that moment of evening when the light and the darkness are so evenly balanced that the constraint of day and the suspense of night neutralize each other, leaving absolute mental liberty. [p. 107]

Tess knows nature as a child of the folk. But, because of her self-consciousness (a more exact term for her dreaminess), she recognizes the earth as the ground level of value in a more than instinctual way. Her verbalizations of her reveries are examples of a consciousness beyond the blindly intuitive. While unconsciously "her quiescent glide was of a piece with the element she moved in," and she "an integral part of the scene," Tess's predisposition for self-recognition individualizes her:

At times her whimsical fancy would intensify natural processes around her till they seemed a part of her own story. Rather they became a part of it; for the world is only a psychological phenomenon, and what they seemed they were. . . .

But this encompassment of her own characterization, based on shreds of convention, peopled by phantoms and voices antipathetic to her, was a sorry and mistaken creation of Tess's fancy—a cloud of moral hobgoblins by which she was terrified without reason. It was they that were out of harmony with the actual world, not she. Walking among the sleeping birds in the hedges, watching the skipping rabbits on a moonlit warren, or standing under a pheasant-laden bough, she

looked upon herself as a figure of Guilt intruding into
the haunts of Innocence. But all the while she was
making a distinction where there was no difference.
Feeling herself in antagonism, she was quite in accord. She had been made to break an accepted social
law, but no law known to the environment in which
she fancied herself such an anomaly. [p. 108]

The artist's consciousness apprehends the earth and the
workings of nature as the foundation of value. But, because
his insight is necessarily self-conscious, his imagination must
recreate the original catalysts to his perception, a group of
alienated figures battling on grounds similar to his own.
Dorothy Van Ghent's view of the novel is invaluable in its
comprehensiveness:

The naturalistic premise of the book—the condition of
earth in which life is placed—is the most obvious,
fundamental, and inexorable of facts; but because it
is the physically "given," into which and beyond which
there can be no penetration, it exists as mystery; it is
thus, even as the basis of all natural manifestation, itself of the quality of the supernatural. . . . The folk
are the bridge between mere earth and moral individuality; of the earth as they are, separable conscious ego
does not arise among them to weaken animal instinct
and confuse response—it is the sports, the deracinated
ones, like Tess and Clare and Alec, who are morally
individualized and who are therefore able to suffer isolation, alienation, and abandonment, or to make others
so suffer; the folk, while they remain folk, cannot be
individually isolated, alienated, or lost, for they are
amoral and their existence is colonial rather than personal.[4]

Tess, even in her conventional desire to baptize her baby
before the infant dies, reveals her tragic rebelliousness in
her self-made ritual: "if Providence would not ratify such

4. Ibid., pp. 204–05.

an act of approximation she, for one, did not value the
kind of heaven lost by the irregularity—either for herself
or for her child" (p. 120). Both Tess and Clare must cast
off the hindrances of past attachments: Tess, with a growing self-assertion beyond conventional social and religious
codes as well as rural superstitions (in her rejection of her
mother's advice and her ironic acceptance of Angel's ag-
nosticism); Clare, with the personal faith developed only
after he deserts his wife. Angel finally overcomes in actuality what he once considered he had overcome by thought
alone. When Tess sets off for Talbothays dairy, "some spirit
rose automatically as the sap in the twigs"; in spite of her
social handicap, she still "was unexpended youth, surging
up anew after its temporary check, and bringing with it
hope, and the invincible instinct towards self-delight" (p.
127), just as Cain himself (one of Hardy's favorite mythic
allusions), in Byron's words, sees nothing

> To make death hateful, save an innate clinging,
> A loathsome, and yet all invincible
> Instinct of life, which I abhor, as I
> Despise myself, yet cannot overcome—
> And so I live. Would I had never lived! [5]

Like Clym Yeobright, Angel Clare is an idealized intellectual, a modern man whose age is measured by the intensity of his experience, and yet whose only experience
until marriage has been thought, that "disease of flesh."
By the time he wrote *Tess,* however, Hardy makes clear the
limitations of a Clym in the responsibility he assigns to
Angel's dangerous shortsightedness. Clare, like Sue Bridehead, has all the intellectual qualifications for being "advanced," but breaks down when his ideals are confronted
by experience. He is the opposite of Jude Fawley, who
gains modern consciousness in the first place from the destruction of his conventional thinking and beliefs by direct
experience. When Clare first appears, there is, as in Tess,
something "nebulous, preoccupied, vague, in his bearing"

5. Byron, *Cain,* I, i, 111–15.

(p. 147). He possesses an "intellectual liberty" (p. 151) that has prevented him, unlike his brothers, from going to Cambridge. He is the counterpart to Tess's "absolute mental liberty"—that is, as in the relation between Clym and Eustacia, his intellectual knowledge is the conceptual complement to its dramatic expression in his future wife. Tess feels what he thinks:

> He was surprised to find this young woman—who though but a milkmaid had just that touch of rarity about her which might make her the envied of her housemates—shaping such sad imaginings. She was expressing in her own native phrases—assisted a little by her Sixth Standard training—feelings which might almost have been called those of the age—*the ache of modernism*. The perception arrested him less when he reflected that what are called advanced ideas are really in great part but the latest fashion in definition—a more accurate expression, by words in *logy* and *ism*, of sensations which men and women have vaguely grasped for centuries. [p. 160; my italics]

We recall the scene on Egdon Heath where modern consciousness was first realized as "the hitherto unrecognized original." With this recognition "the ache of modernism" is born, as we have shown progressively through the novels. In his last books, Hardy has transformed a development only implicit in his early work into an explicit statement. But Clare himself has reached "modernism" only intellectually; before the real recognition is possible, he must submit to experience:

> Still, it was strange that they should have come to her while yet so young; more than strange; it was impressive, interesting, pathetic. Not guessing the cause, there was nothing to remind him that experience is as to intensity, and not as to duration. Tess's passing corporeal blight had been her mental harvest. [p. 160]

We are reminded, too, of the pathetically humorous moments before Tess's confession on the wedding-night, when Angel mournfully avows his two-day spree in London, hardly expecting a tale to issue from Tess's lips that will overpower the whole of his own experience. Like the horizontal landscape that is the scene of Clym and Eustacia's most fulfilling moment, the scenic approach to Talbothays dairy presages the happy beginnings of Tess's love: "the milk oozed forth" "upon the hemmed expanse of verdant *flatness*" (pp. 137, 136). The joyful "strumming" of Angel's harp (!), which breaks the "soundlessness" (p. 157) around Tess, seems to echo Gabriel Oak's flute early in *Far From the Madding Crowd*—an ill omen even then of man's deceptively beautiful intrusion upon nature. Hardy's almost crude, but nonetheless telling, use of the Adam and Eve metaphor in his early novels also recurs (for example, on p. 167), a foreboding presentiment not unlike that of the flute and the harp. Clare's dangerous inexperience also shows itself in his view of Tess "no longer [as] the milkmaid, but a visionary essence of woman" (p. 167), much like the whole subject of Jocelyn Pierston's artistic fancies in *The Well-Beloved* and the inapplicability of those "visions" to actual human relationships.

Tess tries to mediate between the extremes of Angel and Alec, each of whom represents an individualized alienation from the community—one through a surfeit of intellectualism, the other through material overabundance.[6] There are echoes of Troy's "Romanticism" in our awareness of Tess's own acute sense of individuality: "Upon her sensations the whole world depended to Tess; through her existence all her fellow-creatures existed, to her. The universe itself only came into being for Tess on the particular day in the particular year in which she was born" (p. 199). Angel's "alienation" (p. 212)—it is interesting to note Hardy's use of so contemporary a term—lies in his consciousness of a "divergence" from his origins. The vicarage life "futilely attempt[s] to check what wisdom would be content to

6. See Van Ghent, p. 209.

regulate," the "passionate pulse of existence" (p. 203) that he has experienced at Talbothays.

Tess and Angel finally throw off the constraints oppressing their love; but the past soon returns to destroy their bliss. For Tess, "every pulse singing in her ears, was a voice that joined with nature in revolt against her scrupulousness" (p. 228). In spite of her wish to confess before marriage, the " 'appetite for joy' which pervades all creation, that tremendous force which sways humanity to its purpose, as the tide sways the helpless weed, was not to be controlled by vague lucubrations over the social rubric" (p. 244). Thus, the great sin in the world of Hardy's novels is committed anew: "She dismissed the past—trod upon it and put it out, as one treads on a coal that is smouldering and dangerous" (p. 246). Nevertheless, it seems that, no matter the cost, the suffering to come is still part of "that tremendous force which sways humanity to its purpose."

> And now, I think, the meaning of the evolution of civilization is no longer obscure to us. It must present the struggle between Eros and Death, between the instinct of life and the instinct of destruction, as it works itself out in the human species. . . . And it is this battle of the giants that our nursemaids try to appease with their lullaby about Heaven.[7]

The seeds of Angel's late realization and the cost of Tess's suffering are ironically laid out in Clare's thoughts as he regards his bride in the hours before her confession:

> "Do I realize solemnly enough how utterly and irretrievably this little womanly thing is the creature of my good or bad faith and fortune? I think not. I think I could not, unless I were a woman myself. . . . And shall I ever neglect her, or hurt her, or even forget to consider her? God forbid such a crime!" [p. 278]

With Clare's reaction to Tess's confession, Hardy's major concerns in his last two novels become clear: with the quiet

7. Sigmund Freud, *Civilization and Its Discontents*, 21: 122.

and solemn death of the community at the close of *The Woodlanders*, the confrontation within the alienated individual consciousness between natural (or for Hardy as artist, dramatic) impulses, and social (or for Hardy as thinker, conceptual) tendencies becomes the subject of his fiction. After his wife's avowal, Angel "smother[ed] his affection for her" (p. 295). He, like Sue Bridehead, is prevented from *feeling* what he *thinks* is true, while Tess and Jude form a conceptual understanding of their natures only on the basis of actual experience.

> She broke into sobs, and turned her back to him. It would almost have won round any man but Angel Clare. Within the remote depths of his constitution, so gentle and affectionate as he was in general, there lay hidden a hard logical deposit, like a vein of metal in a soft loam, which turned the edge of everything that attempted to traverse it. It had blocked his acceptance of the Church; it blocked his acceptance of Tess. [p. 308]

Clare's selfish behavior toward his wife is an expression of his own divided self, even in the implications of the image of Tess as "Apostolic Charity herself returned to a self-seeking modern world" (p. 309). For Clare, it is "self-seeking" in a literal sense. He causes Tess to suffer because his own inner conflicts proscribe his ability to love. That "disease of flesh" is upon him:

> His thought had been unsuspended; he was becoming ill with thinking; eaten out with thinking; withered by thinking; scourged out of all his former pulsating flexuous domesticity. [p. 310]

Trapped by the problems of identity, he suggests Jocelyn Pierston when the idea flashes upon him that the Tess he once loved was but a fancy of his own selfish imagination:

> Some might risk the odd paradox that with more animalism he would have been the nobler man. We do

not say it. Yet Clare's love was doubtless ethereal to a
fault, imaginative to impracticability. With these natures, corporeal presence is sometimes less appealing
than corporeal absence; the latter creating an ideal
presence that conveniently drops the defects of the
real. She found that her personality did not plead her
cause so forcibly as she had anticipated. The figurative
phrase was true: she was another woman than the one
who had excited his desire. [p. 312]

With the juxtaposed movements of Tess and Angel's
disparate levels of consciousness, the battleground of the
novel becomes "the mutually destructive interdependence
of flesh and spirit." The wandering, anchorless ego must
find its base in an order of its own making, without the
guidance of a community fire: "she was appalled by the determination revealed in the depths of this gentle being she
had married—the will to subdue the grosser to the subtler
emotion, the substance to the conception, the flesh to the
spirit" (p. 313). The "shade of his own limitations" hangs
over both partners as the cause of their suffering (just as
Tess's own dreaminess caused both her meeting with Alec
and her attraction for Angel): "With all his attempted in-
dependence of judgment this advanced and well-meaning
young man, a sample product of the last five-and-twenty
years, was yet the slave to custom and conventionality when
surprised back into his early teachings" (p. 338). The tension engendered by Clare's rootedness in a code that his
intellect rejects forms the background to the details of
Tess's ordeal until their next, and last, meeting.

Meanwhile, Tess exhibits that side of human nature
which is lacking in Angel. "With the shortening of the days
all hope of obtaining her husband's forgiveness began to
leave her; and there was something of the habitude of the
wild animal in the unreflecting instinct with which she
rambled on—disconnecting herself by littles from her event-
ful past at every step, obliterating her identity" (p. 351).
Her tender slaying of the wounded pheasants represents an

identity between herself and concrete symbols of the foundations of her own blossoming perception. It evokes the correspondent extreme to Angel: "She was ashamed of herself for her gloom of the night, based on nothing more tangible than a sense of condemnation under an arbitrary law of society which had no foundation in Nature" (p. 355). At Flintcomb-Ash, the landscape reflects the psychological aspects of the novel: while the earth has previously been seen, especially at Talbothays, as symbolic of fertility and generation, the "starve-acre place" (p. 363) is barren and unyielding. But, still, "the two forces were at work here as everywhere, the inherent will to enjoy, and the circumstantial will against enjoyment" (p. 365).

But "there was a limit to her powers of renunciation" (p. 376). Tess's meeting with the transformed Alec comes, coincidentally, after her decision not to visit Angel's parents once she has arrived in Emminster. D'Urberville's changed appearance as a preacher reinvokes, through Tess's growing perception, the ground level of the novel's value-eye:

> . . . animalism had become fanaticism . . .
>
> The lineaments, as such, seemed to complain. They had been diverted from their hereditary connotation to signify impressions for which nature did not intend them. Strange that their very elevation was a misapplication, that to raise seemed to falsify. [p. 390]

Her final response to him is a portrait of her fate in miniature.

> "Now, punish me!" she said, turning up her eyes to him with the hopeless defiance of the sparrow's gaze before its captor twists its neck. "Whip me, crush me; you need not mind those people under the rick! I shall not cry out. Once victim, always victim—that's the law!" [p. 423]

The scene takes place on the barren fields at Flintcomb-Ash, where the threshing-machine is used artificially to induce greater productivity from barren soil and alienated labor. The symbolism of the machine in the context of the passage is apt:

> "Remember, my lady, I was your master once! I will be your master again. If you are any man's wife, you are mine!"
> The threshers now began to stir below. [p. 423]

And yet Tess's return to Alec is in accord with the finally amoral "naturalistic premise" of the book, as symbolized by the earth. She submits, willingly or not, to the inexorable final cause and touchstone that informs the fictional universe, both in this fatal event as well as in her moments of illumination. If the earth embodies the essential oneness achieved in her deepest moments of dreaminess and desire, it is also the source of her greatest pains. It is "decisive in the final event of Tess's tragedy—her return to Alec, for Alec provides her at least a place to go." [8]

Meanwhile, Angel has realized that Tess's sins "were not sins of intention, but of inadvertence,[9] and [asks] why should she have been punished so persistently?" (p. 454). "His inconsistencies rushed upon him in a flood" (p. 435), and he finally assumes responsibility for her suffering. In his travels, Clare has met a mysterious stranger whose death climaxes the wisdom he imparts to his young companion:

> The stranger had sojourned in many more lands and among many more peoples than Angel; to his cosmopolitan mind such deviations from the social norm [as Tess's], so immense to domesticity, were no more than are the irregularities of vale and mountain-chain to the whole terrestrial curve. [p. 433]

Or,

> Thus, judging by bulk of effect, it becomes impossible to estimate the intrinsic value of ideas, acts, material

8. Van Ghent, p. 203. See the full discussion of this aspect of the "naturalistic premise," pp. 202–03.

9. Cf. Lucetta's "laxity of inadvertence rather than of intention" in *The Mayor of Casterbridge*.

things: we are forced to appraise them by the curves of their career. [*Life,* p. 172]

What is crucial is the nature of the perceptive eye that judges: "he had asked himself why he had not judged Tess constructively rather than biographically, by the will rather than by the deed" (p. 473). Angel, too late, achieves the artist's consciousness, while Tess has lived out its tragic reality by suffering the consequences of his previous limitations. At their pitiful reunion, "[b]oth seemed to implore something to shelter them from reality" (p. 484). Their few days of freedom together are granted only at the ultimate cost, the final payment for transgressing, in mind as well as in deed, the conventions of the so-called community. For the too-conscious there is no reward, "for nothing has ever been more unendurable to man and to human society than freedom!" [10]

10. Fyodor Dostoyevsky, *The Brothers Karamazov* (Baltimore, Md.. 1964), p. 296.

7 *Jude the Obscure*

Jude the Obscure, Hardy's finest novel, is stark and austere, "a series of seemings, or personal impressions" (1895 preface) clear and uncluttered in a way unique in his work. The book marks his furthest advance in fiction on two fronts: in its structure and style, and in the nature of its subject. Hardy approaches the portrayal of consciousness and the power of man's inner world in his strongest anticipations of the coming experimenters in the art of fiction, and tells, "without a mincing of words, of a deadly war waged beween flesh and spirit; . . . the tragedy of unfulfilled aims" (1895 preface). For the first time, there are no intruders upon the Wessex scene. And although the book takes place in Wessex (except for the scenes in Christminster), the character of the rural community, even as it is seen in *Tess,* is completely transformed. *Jude* is a novel modern in its assumptions, for Wessex is now as barren a home for its inhabitants as a city. The novel works toward its one test of human fulfillment, perhaps the final test in Hardy's fiction, in Jude and Sue Bridehead's experiment. The test is failed and we must ask why in order to discover the artist's underlying statement about the dialectic of men and nature in the form of society.

After *The Mayor of Casterbridge,* the last of the novels in which the central figure is known mostly through his actions, Hardy began to interest himself primarily in the inner lives of his characters; as a result, he initiated a series of hesitant attempts to find a way of meeting the demands of his imagination in a narrative direction. We have seen, for example, his interest in perspectives in the window-imagery in *The Woodlanders,* and the development of his characters' self-consciousness from Troy's "Romanticism" to Tess and Angel's awakenings. With *Jude,* style and subject become interwoven, as the content of his concerns necessarily dictates the manner of their portrayal. The tension in style apparent in all his novels is nowhere so relieved—and, at the same time, nowhere so acute—as in *Jude,* where, despite his achievement of an often direct manner of narrative and dialogue,[1] the direction introduced by the artist demands more than his powers of dramatic execution can handle. David Daiches's comments on Hardy exactly reveal the tension between the content of his insights and the manner in which they are expressed. Hardy is now seen, by contrasting the questions in our study with Daiches's, as a figure bridging the old public world and the modern inner world:

> Even Hardy, a novelist devastatingly critical of the assumptions of his age, carries his plots forward by public symbols, and it is worth considering the parts played in *The Mayor of Casterbridge, Tess of the D'Urbervilles,* and *Jude the Obscure* by marrying and giving in marriage, gain or loss of fortune, failure or success in social ambition.

In his address to these questions in the content of his novels, Hardy is an eminent example of "the ache of modernism" that preceded the work of the artists of Daiches's study—artists who owed their freedom, in a real way, to the inner decay of Wessex. Again, in describing developments after Hardy, Daiches speaks of problems crucial to the late novels, especially *Jude:*

> The modern novelist (in the sense in which the term is being used in this book)[2] is born when such public machinery is no longer used in order to achieve the plot-

---

1. For example, the bedroom scene when Arabella tells Jude that she is not really pregnant:

"There's nothing to tell. I made a mistake."
"What?"
"It was a mistake."
He sat bolt upright in bed and looked at her. [p. 70]

2. Here lies the exclusion of Hardy from his discussion.

pattern, and the true inwardness of a character's moral and psychological problems can be revealed only by removing him from the distorting mirror of a public sense of significance and exploring the truth about him in an isolation either real or symbolic.

Jude the Obscure is the only novel in which plot, the essence of Hardy's fiction in the past, is superseded by what the artist himself calls "a series of seemings."

Are human relations really possible, or is every individual condemned ultimately to remain in the prison of his own incorrigibly private consciousness? [3]

It is this question that *Jude* must answer for Hardy. Perhaps it is enough that the late novels have even brought us far enough to pose these problems; yet *Jude* does attempt to resolve them.

The setting of Jude's abortive suicide attempt is almost an allegory of literary history. It is as though the water is still frozen enough for Jude to have to live until the thaw of discovery. The following juxtaposition of passages, Jude's suicide scene and Stein's words in *Lord Jim,* may be used to illustrate the point:

> Jude put one foot on the edge of the ice, and then the other: it cracked under his weight; but this did not deter him. He ploughed his way inward to the centre, the ice making sharp noises as he went. When just about the middle he looked around him and gave a jump. The cracking repeated itself; but he did not go down. He jumped again, but the cracking had ceased. Jude went back to the edge, and stepped upon the ground.
>
> It was curious, he thought. What was he reserved for? [p. 82]

> "Yes! Very funny this terrible thing is. A man that is born falls into a dream like a man who falls into the sea. If he tries to climb out into the air as inexperi-

3. David Daiches, *The Novel and the Modern World*, p. 26.

enced people endeavour to do, he drowns—*nicht wahr?*
. . . No! I tell you! The way is to the destructive element submit yourself, and with the exertions of your
hands and feet in the water make the deep, deep sea
keep you up. So if you ask me—how to be?" [4]

In *Tess,* consciousness itself became the battleground of
the novel. Tess and Angel each experienced that "mutually
destructive interdependence of flesh and spirit," and together presented the possibilities of human relations within
the condition that each was imprisoned within the cell of
his own ego. With *Jude,* the entire novel focuses finally on
its central character: Hardy has combined, in a single figure,
the intellectual needs of Angel and the fleshy humanity of
Tess. The conditions of his isolation are, as in our first
views of Tess, already latent in his family history and early
life. His gradual and painful discoveries are those of the
wandering ego whose consciousness of its own anchorlessness
defines the meaning of *modern.* These are the preconditions
upon which Joyce, the epic poet of the coming century, was
to attempt to build anew:

> We are alone. Come. And the voices say with them:
> We are your kinsmen. And the air is thick with their
> company as they call to me, their kinsman, making
> ready to go, shaking the wings of their exultant and
> terrible youth.
>   . . . Amen. So be it. Welcome, O life! I go to en-
> counter for the millionth time the reality of experience
> and to forge in the smithy of my soul the uncreated
> conscience of my race.[5]

Early in *Jude,* Hardy describes moments of perceptive
flashes, almost "epiphanies," in the mind of Jude Fawley as
a child. As the boy stares down into the well at Marygreen,
we see, in the artist's traditional diction,

4. Joseph Conrad, *Lord Jim* (New York, 1921), p. 214.
5. James Joyce, *A Portrait of the Artist as a Young Man* (New
York, 1965), pp. 252–53.

his face wearing the fixity of a thoughtful child's who felt the pricks of life somewhat before his time.

But, for a moment, the usual style blends with a startling symbolic transformation:

> The well into which he was looking was as ancient as the village itself, and from his present position appeared as a long circular perspective ending in a shining disk of quivering water at a distance of a hundred feet down. [p. 5]

When we learn that "the well-shaft was probably the only relic of the local history that remained absolutely unchanged" (p. 6), the child's portrait embodies an entire historical movement. As the youthful product of contemporary civilization, Jude dimly catches sight of "the hitherto unrecognized original" beneath the constantly changing face of a landscape that, even in Wessex, reflects the renunciative labor of centuries. Even more striking is another passage from Jude's childhood; visual imagery (light and dark, mists and fog, and, of course, twilight) is slowly intertwined symbolically with the movement of his perceptive eye, his consciousness:

> The fog had by this time become more translucent, and the position of the sun could be seen through it. He pulled his straw hat over his face, and peered through the interstices of the plaiting at the white brightness, vaguely reflecting. Growing up brought responsibilities, he found. Events did not rhyme quite as he had thought. Nature's logic was too horrid for him to care for. That mercy towards one set of creatures was cruelty towards another sickened his sense of harmony.

Then, with a sudden shift incredible in Hardy:

> As you got older, and felt yourself to be at the centre of your time, and not at a point in its circumference, as you had felt when you were little, you were seized with a sort of shuddering, he perceived. All around you

there seemed to be something glaring, garish, rattling, and the noises and glares hit upon the little cell called your life, shook it, and warped it. [p. 15]

The cell of the young Jude's consciousness—isolation is an assumed fact in the fictional universe now, the beginning, not the end, of the novel's movement—is shaken by the calls both of the spirit and the flesh. His infatuation with Christminster stems from his early affection for his schoolmaster, Philloston; it is "the new Jerusalem" of learning and advancement that first provides him with "a tangibility, a permanence, a hold on his life" (p. 20). That this attraction, like the other, springs from a freedom of choice is, of course, negated right away; instead, "[i]t had been a yearning of his heart to find something to anchor on, to cling to—for some place which he could call admirable" (p. 24). His new hope is expressed in the imagery of light:

Through the intervening fortnight [when Physician Vilbert is to bring him grammars in return for orders] he ran about and smiled outwardly at his inward thoughts, as if they were people meeting and nodding to him—smiled with that singularly beautiful irradiation which is seen to spread on young faces at the inception of some glorious idea, as if a supernatural lamp were held inside their transparent natures, giving rise to the flattering fancy that heaven lies about them then. [p. 28]

The revelation of the power of the flesh seizes him when he is older, though still the dreamy boy with intellectual pretensions. When he first sees Arabella, the attraction is involuntary in an even stronger way than his first desire for anchorage:

for somehow or other the eyes of the brown girl rested in his own when he had said the words, and there was a momentary flash of intelligence, a dumb announcement of affinity *in posse,* between herself and him, which, so far as Jude Fawley was concerned, had no sort of pre-meditation in it. She saw that he had singled her out from the three, as a woman is singled out in such cases, for no reasoned purpose of further acquaintance, but in commonplace obedience to conjunctive orders from headquarters, unconsciously received by unfortunate men when the last intention of their lives is to be occupied with the feminine. [p. 43]

The directing impulses are within—"headquarters" is sex, the latent, but directive, store of energy that has found progressively explicit expression since the early heath scenes in *The Return of the Native*. There was

something in her quite antipathetic to that side of him which had been occupied with literary study and the magnificent Christminster dream. . . . He saw this with his intellectual eye, just for a short fleeting while, as by the light of a falling lamp one might momentarily see an inscription on a wall before being enshrouded in darkness. [pp. 45–46]

The imagery is consistent throughout the novels, finding its clearest, simplest expression here. Jude begins to learn the determinism of the real as opposed to the wishful; it is

a new thing, a great hitch . . . in the gliding and noiseless current of his life, and he felt as a snake must feel who has sloughed off its winter skin, and cannot understand the brightness and sensitiveness of its new one. [p. 47]

In short, as if materially, a compelling arm of extraordinary muscular power seized hold of him—something which had nothing in common with the spirits and influences that had moved him hitherto. This seemed to care little for his reason and his will, nothing for his so-called elevated intentions, and moved him along, as a violent schoolmaster a schoolboy he has seized by the collar, in a direction which tended towards the embrace of a woman for whom he had no

respect, and whose life had nothing in common with
his own except locality. [p. 48]

And except for the attractions of sex—nature is the ground
level here, as in *Tess;* but it disappears as a touchstone of
value to function instead as the indifferent, though determining, factor of sexual instinct. "These impulses in themselves are neither good nor bad. We classify them and their
expressions in that way, according to their relation to the
needs and demands of the human community." [6]

Jude marries Arabella because she has told him she is
pregnant: "He knew well, too well, in the secret centre of
his brain, that Arabella was not worth a great deal as a
specimen of womankind. Yet, such being the custom of the
rural districts among honourable young men who had
drifted so far into intimacy with a woman as he unfortu-
nately had done, he was ready to abide by what he had said,
and take the consequences" (p. 65). In this action, Jude unconsciously responds in accordance with the code of a
community that he takes for granted. But when he learns
that the pregnancy was a sham, his consciousness is awakened:

When Jude awoke the next morning he seemed to see
the world with a different eye. As to the point in question he was compelled to accept her word; in the circumstances he could not have acted otherwise while
ordinary notions prevailed.

But now the question:

But how came they to prevail?
There seemed to him, vaguely and dimly, something
wrong in a social ritual which made necessary a cancel-
ling of well-formed schemes involving years of thought
and labour, of foregoing a man's one opportunity of
showing himself superior to the lower animals, and of

6. Sigmund Freud, *Thoughts for the Times on War and Death,*
14: 281.

contributing his units of work to the general progress
of his generation because of a momentary surprise by
a new and transitory instinct which had nothing in it
of the nature of vice, and could be only at the most
called weakness. He was inclined to inquire what he
had done, or she lost, for that matter, that he deserved
to be caught in a gin which would cripple him, if not
her also, for the rest of a lifetime? [pp. 70–71]

Jude's impetus for finally going to Christminster once
he and his wife have separated is "more nearly related to
the emotional side of him than to the intellectual" (p. 90).
He involuntarily acts in accordance with a drive closer to
the now-familiar reality of the flesh (the impulse that lets
him carry out in action his spiritual desires which, even by
now, are implicitly effete by contrast) than to the dream
surrounding his original interest in the city of learning. It is
as though he had fallen in love with Sue Bridehead before
meeting her. Christminster is "within hail of the Wessex
border" (p. 90); but, by now, the implications in *Tess* that
locality is irrelevant to the pervasive conditions of social
existence are clearly operative.

Still, Jude's arrival in the city makes the intimations of
his isolation plain. In answer to why his suicide attempt
failed, he begins to realize that he is in search of himself:
"Knowing not a human being here, Jude began to be impressed with the isolation of his own personality, as with a
self-spectre, the sensation being that of one who walked but
could not make himself seen or heard" (p. 92). Along with
an awareness of the inner question come corresponding
changes in his outer perception: the reality of his marital
isolation had created questions of social forms; an even
more complete isolation confronts him now as he discovers
the concrete reality of his intellectual dream. On seeing the
crumbling colleges, "[i]t seemed impossible that modern
thought could house itself in such decrepit and superseded
chambers" (p. 92).

The law of Jude's perception—perhaps the reason he is
Hardy's fullest, most living character—is that consciousness

grows with the accumulation of actual experience, that real awareness is the result only of real experience. While the artist has, so far, tried to meet the stylistic demands of his subject, he breaks down into an explicit narrative overview at those crucial moments when, because of his limitations, he can hold the novel together only by stepping in himself:

> For a moment there fell on Jude a true illumination; that here in the stone yard was a centre of effort as worthy as that dignified by the name of scholarly study within the noblest of the colleges. But he lost it under stress of his old idea. He would accept any employment which might be offered him on the strength of his late employer's recommendation; but he would accept it as a provisional thing only. This was his form of the modern vice of unrest. [p. 98]

Hardy cannot let his characters wholly define his world because he is forced to demolish the old assumptions at the same time that he searches for new ones to take their place. The artist is not yet ready to be "refined out of existence" because of his own uncertainties. As a result, the distinction between character and creator must emerge at critical directive moments like this, as the passage continues:

> Moreover he perceived that at best only copying, patching and imitating went on here; which he fancied to be owing to some temporary and local cause. He did not at that time see that mediaevalism was as dead as a fern-leaf in a lump of coal; that other developments were shaping in the world around him, in which Gothic architecture and its associations had no place. The deadly animosity of contemporary logic and vision towards so much of what he held in reverence was not yet revealed to him. [pp. 98-99]

One feels as if Hardy were about to lower Jude's fate upon him from above (Swinburne wrote to the author after the book's publication: "But, if I may say so, how cruel you are!" *Life*, p. 270). It is here that Hardy's work again exemplifies a bridge between the old narrative sensibility and the dictates of the new. We feel his constant effort to sink his own insights into the stuff of the drama, and not to let them press down conceptually from an omniscient consciousness.

At this point Sue Bridehead appears. D. H. Lawrence points out how the need that Sue fulfills in Jude allows Hardy's meaning to work fully through the drama inself:

> By creating a vacuum, she could cause the vivid flow which clarified him. By arousing him, by drawing from him his turgid vitality, made thick and heavy and physical with Arabella, she could bring into consciousness that which he contained. For he was heavy and full of unrealized life, clogged with untransmuted knowledge, with accretion of his senses. His whole life had been till now an indrawing, ingestion.

> [Sue causes him] to find conscious expression for that which he held in his blood . . . to transmute his sensuous being into another state, a state of clarity, of consciousness.[7]

Thus, she is the catalyst for the tragedy that was potential even before her appearance; the only element needed to transform the existing conditions of Jude's life into explicit modern tragedy is his consciousness of the essence of those conditions—his frustration. "The consciousness of her living presence stimulated him" (p. 104) before he ever talked to her. From the moment he confronts Sue eye-to-eye (before he is known to her as her cousin), "the emotion which had been accumulating in his breast as the bottled-up effect of solitude and the poetized locality he dwelt in, insensibly began to precipitate itself on this half-visionary form" (p. 105). In spite of the "enormous reasons why he must not attempt intimate acquaintance with Sue Bridehead now that his interest in her had shown itself to be unmistakably of a sexual kind, [his desire] loomed as stubbornly as ever. But it was also obvious that man could not live by work

7. D. H. Lawrence, "Study of Thomas Hardy," in *Selected Literary Criticism,* pp. 209–210, pp. 210–211.

alone; that the particular man Jude, at any rate, wanted something to love" (p. 114).

Angel Clare's great fault lay in his intellectual or conceptual eye for the knowledge of generalities and his corresponding ignorance, even scorn, for the particulars of experience. But, as we have seen, Jude gains consciousness from direct experience alone. While he has even questioned the origins of the social code, the experience that prompted the question was a receptive one. It is not until he yearns to give his love to Sue, who calls directly to his own "unrealized life," that he opens himself, as Angel finally does, to the reality of emotional pain. Jude can know the general only through the particular: his real discovery of his own isolation begins in Christminster, his consciousness before only vague and dim. In his experience with Sue, Jude comes to know directly the effects of society upon what is natural in man; only then does he come to an intellectual awareness of the effects and the reality of civilization itself. With Sue's marriage to Philloston, he feels for the first time "the terrible sickness of hopeless, handicapped love" (p. 128); his isolation is even heavier now that he is "[d]eprived of the objects of both intellect and emotion" (p. 141). He seems to expect to find relief by retreating into Wessex. But of course the reality of the world is now, more than ever, psychological:

> Refreshed by some breakfast, he went up to his old room and lay down in his shirt-sleeves, after the manner of the artizan. He fell asleep for a short while, and when he awoke it was as if he had awakened in hell. It *was* hell—"the hell of conscious failure," both in ambition and in love. He thought of that previous abyss into which he had fallen before leaving this part of the country; the deepest deep he had supposed it then; but it was not so deep as this. That had been the breaking in of the outer bulwarks of his hope: this was of his second line. [p. 147]

At this point, Jude begins to chastise himself. He looks to religious renunciation as a means of cleansing the personal scheme that he now fears "had degenerated to, even though it might not have originated in, a social unrest which had no foundation in the nobler instincts; which was purely an artificial product of civilization" (p. 153). He is "full of the superstitions of his belief" (p. 156); yet, in spite of both his stifled physical desire and his intellectual divergence from Sue, "he could scarcely believe that time, creed, or absence, would ever divide him from her" (p. 184). Sue's narcissism and her fear of the physical become known to us mostly through their effect upon Jude. Still, Hardy grants us small glimpses of direct insight into her, such as her early unawareness of her attraction for both Jude and Philloston, and her detached interest in her cousin, like one's interest in "a man puzzling out his way along a labyrinth from which one had one's self escaped" (p. 163). Meanwhile, the frustration between them continues to build; at one of their meetings before living together,

> By every law of nature and sex a kiss was the only rejoinder that fitted the mood and the moment, under the suasion of which Sue's undemonstrative regard of him might not inconceivably have changed its temperature. . . . [But] Jude did not.
> . . . Such intercourse as that would have to content him for the remainder of his life. The lesson of renunciation it was necessary and proper that he, as a parish priest, should learn. [pp. 189–90]

But as the physical and emotional frustrations increase, Jude's consciousness also begins to grow. The tension between the lovers intensifies as "the antagonisms of sex to sex were left without any counterpoising predilections" (p. 199), because the conflict is, really, that of "the mutually destructive interdependence of flesh and spirit." Sue responds to Jude as an agent of his own consciousness; she is, like Eustacia, "an epicure in emotions" (p. 207), though without the counterbalancing sensuousness. In his desperate attempt to suppress the "earthiness" he becomes "ashamed

of" (p. 149), Jude pushes more and more towards an awareness of the chains that bind him. He gives up the idea of
becoming a priest as "he perceived with despondency that,
taken all round, he was a man of too many passions to make
a good clergyman; the utmost he could hope for was that in
a life of constant internal warfare between flesh and spirit
the former might not always be victorious" (p. 231). What
might be termed a self-destructive impulse in Jude is but
the involuntary means by which his experience slams him
against the walls of his cell, calling upon him to recognize
the meaning of that experience. He feels "a growing im-
patience of faith" (p. 235) and longs to see her again and
again.

Their conversations provide some of the best passages in
the novel, especially the episodes before Sue finally agrees
to sleep with Jude and after the death of the children. It is
in these moments that Hardy most forcefully explores the
possibilities of human relations in the context of the given
nature of consciousness within the present social mould.
The dialogue furnishes momentary flashes of illumination at
increasing levels of intensity. After Jude's disillusionment
at visiting the composer of the church hymn, he finds that
Sue, too, has felt the music to be moving:

> "It is odd," she said, in a voice quite changed, "that
> I should care about that air; because——"
> "Because what?"
> "I am not that sort—quite."
> "Not easily moved?"
> "I didn't quite mean that."
> "O, but you are one of that sort, for you are just like
> me at heart!"
> "But not at head."
> She played on, and suddenly turned round; and by
> an unpremeditated instinct each clasped the other's
> hand again.
> She uttered a forced little laugh as she relinquished
> his quickly. "How funny!" she said. "I wonder what
> we both did that for?"

"I suppose because we are both alike, as I said before."

"Not in our thoughts! Perhaps a little in our feelings."

"And they rule thoughts." [pp. 242–43]

Jude's reflections drive him to deeper questioning: " 'Is it . . . that women are to blame; or is it the artificial system of things, under which the normal sex-impulses are turned into devilish domestic gins and springs to noose and hold back those who want to progress?' " (p. 261). In a note to Jude, Sue touches upon the central fact responsible for the possibility of modern tragedy, self-consciousness: "No poor woman has ever wished more than I that Eve had not fallen, so that (as the primitive Christians believed) some harmless mode of vegetation might have peopled Paradise" (pp. 270–71).

Other conversations, too, confront central issues in the novel. The dialogue between Phillotson and his friend Gillingham lays out in a more detached and direct manner the painful discoveries of the lovers. Phillotson, of course, speaks from experience when he talks about granting his wife freedom:

". . . I am simply going to act by instinct, and let principles take care of themselves. . . ."

"But—you see, there's the question of neighbours and society—what will happen if everybody——"

"O, I am not going to be a philosopher any longer! I only see what is under my eyes."

. . . "But if people did as you want to do, there'd be a general domestic disintegration. The family would no longer be the social unit. . . . It will upset all received opinion hereabout. Good God—what will Shaston say?"

"I don't say that it won't. I don't know—I don't know! . . . As I say, I am only a feeler, not a reasoner." [pp. 277–79]

This discussion, and more talk between Jude and Sue them-selves, lay the groundwork for the "experiment" the two will undertake. Sue's utter conventionality, in spite of her opinions, begins to appear even before the test itself. She tells Jude,

> "I fear I am doing you a lot of harm. Ruining your prospects of the Church; ruining your progress in your trade; everything!"
> "The Church is no more to me. . . . My point of bliss is not upward, but here." [p. 285]

Their mental roles are already becoming reversed; he is able, even now, to pronounce the same judgments upon her that he will proclaim with conviction late in the novel: "I think you are incapable of real love" (p. 289). And she can confess her own limitations more rationally now than later, when she will be at the mercy of real experience: "I haven't the courage of my views" (p. 290). But Jude yearns for the test ("Crucify me, if you will! You know you are all the world to me, whatever you do!", p. 290) even though he is aware of the situation ("You concede nothing to me and I have to concede everything to you," p. 292).

Arabella's reappearance forces Sue's submission to Jude, an act springing from rivalry rather than from love. Indeed, Sue conceives of a physical relationship in terms of battle: "I agree! I do love you. I ought to have known that you would conquer in the long run, living like this" (p. 321). And, pointing to the differences arising between them:

> "The little bird is caught at last!" she said, a sadness showing in her smile.
> "No—only nested," he assured her. [p. 322]

Jude sees their union as natural, she, as a socially produced imposition akin to being "licensed to be loved on the prem-ises" (p. 312). Arabella, who is easily misjudged under the cloud of intellectual pretensions surrounding the protago-nists earlier in the novel, demonstrates an intelligence that derives from her intimate contact with the ways of sex; especially when Sue asserts

> "He is mine, if you come to that!"
> "He wasn't yesterday." [p. 212]

An index of the changes that take place in Jude is his shifting opinion about children. While Sue was living with Philloston, he was disgusted at the thought that his beloved's children would also be the schoolmaster's: "Every desired renewal of an existence is debased by being half alloy" (p. 212). But experience has wrought a new attitude that surfaces with the arrival of Little Father Time:

> "The beggarly question of parentage—what is it, after all? What does it matter, when you come to think of it, whether a child is yours by blood or not? All the little ones of our time are collectively the children of us adults of the time, and entitled to our general care. That excessive regard of parents for their own children, and their dislike of other people's, is like class-feeling, patriotism, save-your-own-soulism, and other virtues, a mean exclusiveness at bottom." [p. 330]

Jude and Arabella's child, a crude symbol that is amazingly effective, embodies the fate of the protagonists in an ironic twist of parentage and final circumstance. Father Time is the product of a civilization that has bled humanity from Sue and that has imprisoned each of the lovers in his own private world. In the same way that Jude suffers by giving Sue unrequited love, his child, carrying still further the mutilation of natural impulses by history, is the vehicle of her breakdown. He is the abiding and even more tragic refinement of an already acute self-consciousness. Father Time

> was Age masquerading as Juvenility, and doing it so badly that his real self showed through crevices. A ground swell from ancient years of night seemed now and then to lift the child in this his morning-life, when his face took a back view over some great Atlantic of

Time, and appeared not to care about what it saw.
[p. 332]

The son returns to haunt the father, to confront Jude
with yet another expression of himself and, finally, to complete his fate by precipitating Sue's breakdown. While there
is an intervening period of happiness, it is granted only
while the repressed lies dormant. The Albrickham populace
unobtrusively begins to express its feelings about Jude, Sue,
and the children ("an oppressive atmosphere began to en-
circle their souls," p. 360), at the time when Arabella sees
them at the fair.

When all the elements of past suffering converge on the
couple, they seek refuge in Christminster. There, in a public
confession that, even in this novel, seems to presage final
downfall in Hardy, Jude's words convey the essence of these
final moments:

"I was, perhaps, after all, a paltry victim to the spirit
of mental and social restlessness, that makes so many
unhappy in these days!"

"Don't tell them that!" whispered Sue with tears, at
perceiving Jude's state of mind. "You weren't that. You
struggled nobly to acquire knowledge, and only the
meanest souls in the world would blame you!"

Jude shifted the child into a more easy position on
his arm, and concluded: "And what I appear, a sick
and poor man, is not the worst of me. I am in a chaos
of principles—groping in the dark—acting by instinct
and not after example. Eight or nine years ago when I
came here first, I had a neat stock of fixed opinions,
but they dropped away one by one; and the further I
get the less sure I am. I doubt if I have anything more
for my present rule of life than following inclinations
which do me and nobody else any harm, and actually
give pleasure to those I love best. . . . I perceive there
is something wrong somewhere in our social formulas:
what it is can only be discovered by men or women

with greater insight than mine,—if, indeed, they ever
discover it—at least in our time." [pp. 393–94]

The question is clear: has Hardy moved a bit nearer to
the possibility of hope (past "ever discover it" to a future
potential?) than in *Tess,* where he looked for "a closer interaction of the social machinery than that which now jolts
us round and along; but [where, at least then] such completeness is not to be prophesied, or even conceived as possible"?

The final catastrophe, the hanging of the children by
Father Time and Sue's breakdown, comes after Jude's
speech. According to the doctor ("an advanced man," but
one who can give no consolation), the boy "is the beginning
of the coming universal wish not to live" (p. 406):

> The boy's face expressed the whole tale of their situa-
> tion. On that little shape had converged all the inau-
> spiciousness and shadow which had darkened the first
> union of Jude, and all the accidents, mistakes, fears,
> errors of the last. He was their nodal point, their focus,
> their expression in a single term. For the rashness of
> those parents he had groaned, for their ill-assortment
> he had quaked, and for the misfortunes of these he
> had died. [p. 406]

The final judgment still hangs within the drama, as Jude
and Sue confront each other in the aftermath of the
tragedy:

> Vague and quaint imaginings had haunted Sue in the
> days when her intellect scintillated like a star, that the
> world resembled a stanza or melody composed in a
> dream; it was wonderfully excellent to the half-aroused
> intelligence, but hopelessly absurd at the full waking;
> . . . that at the framing of the terrestrial conditions
> there seemed never to have been contemplated such a
> development of emotional perceptiveness among the
> creatures subject to those conditions as that reached
> by educated and thinking humanity. But affliction

makes opposing forces loom anthropomorphous; and
those ideas were now exchanged for a sense of Jude and
herself fleeing from a persecutor.

"We must conform!" she said mournfully. . . .
"There is no choice. We must. It is no use fighting
against God!"

"It is only against man and senseless circumstance,"
said Jude. [p. 413]

The extent of Hardy's progress in the novels is evident both
in his own explicit psychological statement ("affliction makes
opposing forces loom anthropomorphous," a direct insight
that, earlier, would have been only unconscious and, therefore, expressed by metaphor or symbol alone) and in Jude's
lucid tenacity. Later, too, Jude tells Sue that " 'affliction has
brought you to this unreasonable state!' " and asks again,
"[i]s it peculiar to you, or is it common to woman?" (pp.
423–24), a question sustained in Hardy's novels from the
first to the last. Jude's reason searches for hopes and ex-
planations. " 'Perhaps the world is not illuminated enough
for such experiments as ours! Who were we, to think we
could act as pioneers!' " (p. 425). But his *we* is wishful.
Sue confesses that her relationship with him "began in the
selfish and cruel wish to make your heart ache for me without letting mine ache for you" (p. 426). Jude again is utterly
alone, able to acknowledge in truth only " 'the grind of
stern reality!' " (p. 474).

The association of light with what is real, and its appre-
hension by the rational faculties, seems to define Jude's
last important words in the novel. Only a few, it appears,
may be granted the consciousness to forge the uncreated
conscience of the race; as he dies, he rambles on:

"Sue, my Sue—you darling fool—this is almost more
than I can endure! . . . She was once a woman whose
intellect was to mine like a star to a benzoline lamp:
who saw all *my* superstitions as cobwebs that she could
brush away with a word. Then bitter affliction came to
us, and her intellect broke, and she veered round to

darkness. Strange difference of sex, that time and circumstance, which enlarge the views of most men, narrow the views of women almost invariably. And now
the ultimate horror has come—her giving herself like
this to what she loathes, in her enslavement to forms!
—she, so sensitive, so shrinking, that the very wind
seemed to blow on her with a touch of deference. . . .
As for Sue and me when we were at our own best, long
ago—when our minds were clear, and our love of truth
fearless—the time was not ripe for us! Our ideas were
fifty years too soon to be any good to us. And so the
resistance they met with brought reaction in her, and
recklessness and ruin on me!" [pp. 483–84]

But again he is determined to invoke the *we,* to disbelieve
that Sue was, in fact, untouched by his truth. Still, she may
yet love him. Perhaps Arabella is right when she speaks the
last words of the novel, as she was on the day after Sue first
made love with Jude: " 'She's never found peace since she
left his arms, and never will again till she's as he is now!' "
(p. 494). If the possibility of hope lies in man's potential
ability to correct the social mechanism, perhaps to place it
in accord with nature, then the reasons for Sue's narcissism,
as well as the origins of Jude's cell-like consciousness, may
be removed.

But Hardy, as we have seen, has had to keep the distinction between himself and his characters throughout the novel.
Note, for instance, the two following examples, a narrative
aside and one of his remarks on the press reviews of *Jude:*

The purpose of a chronicler of moods and deeds does
not require him to express his personal views upon the
grave controversy above given. [p. 348]

"Tragedy may be created by an opposing environment
either of things inherent in the universe, or of human
institutions. If the former be the means exhibited and
deplored, the writer is regarded as impious; if the latter, as subversive and dangerous; when all the while he

may never have questioned the necessity or urged the non-necessity of either." [*Life,* p. 274]

The conflict within Hardy's mind between his dramatic and conceptual impulses has been marked since *The Return of the Native.* In *Jude the Obscure,* his imagination has driven him to the boundaries of his limitations in the writing of prose while, at the same time, it has rescued this last precarious vision by calling on the creative resources he did possess. That we must search for his final judgment on man, nature, and society in his last work of fiction in a philosophical distinction suggests that he gave up novel-writing for a reason more profound than is usually offered. It seems that the sustained tension during the years in which he fashioned a constantly evolving imaginative universe brought him to an irresolvable, if not unbearable, conflict. Having granted progressive expression to a series of impulses that he at first tried to suppress in his early and middle novels, he was driven to recognize the size of his own prison and to make a choice. The absence of any such discussion in his autobiography is not unusual: it seems, instead, that he would have willfully omitted such talk himself. There are, though, occasional comments in the *Life* which, from an ostensibly disinterested point of view on his part, might indicate signs of such a struggle, as the novels themselves have unquestionably been seen to do. Here, for example, is an entry of 1896, following the publication of *Jude:*

> "September 8. Why true conclusions are not reached, notwithstanding everlasting palaver. Men endeavour to hold to a mathematical consistency in things, instead of recognizing that certain things may both be good and mutually antagonistic." [*Life,* p. 282]

Perhaps Hardy decided to take the advice of his own Elizabeth-Jane who, like himself, watched Michael Henchard drive himself mad:

> the finer movements of her nature found scope in discovering to the narrow-lived ones around her the secret (as she had once learnt it) of making limited oppor-

tunities endurable; which she deemed to consist in the cunning enlargement of microscopic treatment, of those minute forms of satisfaction that offer themselves to everybody not in positive pain; which thus handled, have much of the same inspiriting effect upon life as wider interests cursorily embraced.

Her teaching had a reflex action upon herself, insomuch that she thought she could perceive no great personal difference between being respected in the nether parts of Casterbridge and glorified at the uppermost end of the social world. Her position was, indeed, to a marked degree one that, in the common phrase, afforded much to be thankful for. . . . And in being forced to class herself among the fortunate she did not cease to wonder at the persistence of the unforeseen, when the one to whom such unbroken tranquility had been accorded in the adult stage was she whose youth had seemed to teach that happiness was but the occasional episode in a general drama of pain. [*Mayor*, pp. 385–86]

In a book published in 1895, the same year as *Jude the Obscure*, another writer, at the beginning rather than the end of a certain journey, expressed similar sentiments:

I have often been faced by this objection: "Why, you tell me yourself that my illness is probably connected with my circumstances and the events of my life. You cannot alter these in any way. How do you propose to help me, then?" And I have been able to make this reply: "No doubt fate would find it easier than I do to relieve you of your illness. But you will be able to convince yourself that much will be gained if we succeed in transforming your hysterical misery into common unhappiness. With a mental life that has been restored to health you will be better armed against that unhappiness." [8]

8. Sigmund Freud and Josef Breuer, *Studies on Hysteria*, 2: 305. (This section was written by Freud alone.)

8 Conclusion

When Clym Yeobright asks his mother, "what is doing well?", she reflects but offers no response. Clym himself, however, has already provided an answer earlier in the conversation—he wants to teach men "how to breast the misery they are born to" (*Return*, pp. 208, 207). In a book published just a few years before *The Return of the Native*, Walter Pater had suggested a different conclusion:

> Not the fruit of experience, but experience itself, is the end. A counted number of pulses only is given to us of a variegated, dramatic life. How may we see in them all that is to be seen in them by the finest sense? How shall we pass most swiftly from point to point, and be present always at the focus where the greatest number of vital forces unite in their purest energy?
>
> To burn always with this hard, gemlike flame, to maintain this ecstasy, is success in life.[1]

Yeobright's intellectual assumptions are those of the rationalist who believes that the individual mind can discover some kind of truth. Hardy wrote *The Return of the Native* when he seems to have first approached the question of the nature of the truth-seeking intellect after his discovery of its destructive possibilities in his early novels. We have seen that a new "churchy," or instinctual, basis reinformed a universe devoid of its former emotional strength; head-quarters" was slowly seen to shift to the inner life of the individual. But while Hardy was painfully redefining the premises of his imaginative universe at the cost of a mortal conflict between his lingering conscious faith in reason and his new artistic impulses, Pater had already cut through to the grim awareness that the novelist was to find only in his last prose work:

1. Walter Pater, *The Renaissance* (London, 1897), pp. 249–50.

the whole scope of observation is dwarfed into the narrow chamber of the individual mind. Experience, already reduced to a group of impressions, is ringed round for each one of us by that thick wall of personality through which no real voice has ever pierced on its way to us, or from us to that which we can only conjecture to be without. Every one of those impressions is the impression of the individual in his isolation, each mind keeping as a solitary prisoner its own dream of a world.[2]

With Henry Knight's intrusion upon the order of Wessex, Hardy had dramatized his own loss of faith in an orthodoxy which was itself an expression of a larger communal sensibility. As a vehicle of the power of reason, Knight inadvertently destroyed the community which the artist had at first envisaged as a refuge from the urban world. Clym Yeobright seems originally to have been Hardy's attempt to combine the best of both worlds. But by *The Return of the Native* he had exposed a lack in the rational intellect as well as in the social structure of community. His own consciousness of the dangerous foolishness of Yeobright's rationalism did not really assert itself, however, until the creation of Angel Clare. Adrift, then, between the two sensibilities initially vying for allegiance in his fiction, Hardy finally concentrated his energies in the "means" of a single character, Michael Henchard, rendering the metaphorical heath landscape into the "volcanic" stuff of the mind itself. Recapitulating on an overtly psychological level the thrust of Darwin's work in his realization of the individual's inner dynamic, he undercut the triumph of regarding solely a man's "ends." By the writing of *Jude the Obscure,* even the rich backdrop of natural setting has retreated before the necessities of the self. "All rectifying stabilities have dropped out of sight; and nothing is left but a frustrated aggregate of querulous and disoriented individuals." [3]

2. Ibid., p. 248.
3. John Holloway, *The Victorian Sage,* p. 289.

External nature appears hostile to man during many episodes in the novels because his separation from natural processes is so acute that he is self-alienated as well; the power of exterior nature, which in reality reflects man's inner life, threatens the self-conscious creature by acting as a mirror that reveals what is self-hidden. That artistic perception is a projective mechanism Hardy suggested as early as 1865: "The poetry of a scene varies with the minds of the perceivers. Indeed, it does not lie in the scene at all." By assigning a projective quality only to the poetic sense, however, Hardy implied at the time that the rational sense is something different, something objective. But with the progressive breakdown both of the community and of a viable rational mode of truth-seeking in his novels (though not in his thought), his recognition of the individual mind's isolation forced him implicitly to assign what was originally only an artistic mode of perception—projection—to mental processes in general.

The Well-Beloved, which first appeared in periodicals in 1892 before it was fully published in 1897, is almost a clear avowal of this progression. It is also a rather clear meditation on the nature of art itself, and on the crucial relation between modes of artistic perception and cognitive processes in general. The artist notes in the preface how the book differs from his other fiction: "As for the story itself, it may be worth while to remark that, differing from all or most others of the series in that the interest aimed at is of an ideal or subjective nature, and frankly imaginative, verisimilitude in the sequence of events has been subordinated to the said aim." The subject of the tale is the sculptor Jocelyn Pierston's search for his Well-Beloved, a visionary essence of woman that constantly changes its corporeal incarnation. Pierston is, of course, incapable of reaching outside of himself in any way other than through art.

> Jocelyn threw into plastic creations that ever-bubbling spring of emotion which, without some conduit into space, will surge upwards and ruin all but the greatest

men. It was probably owing to this, certainly not on
account of any care or anxiety for such a result, that he
was successful in his art, successful by a seemingly sudden spurt, which carried him at one bound over the
hindrances of years. [p. 49]

The description is almost autobiographical: Hardy himself
was never ambitious, even though he turned to fiction as
a means of practical success. He had also been prone to
idealism as a child and as a lover. While Pierston is able to
pacify his yearnings in his work, he is plagued by a corresponding "utter domestic loneliness" (p. 50). Whether the
Well-Beloved resides in Marcia Bencomb or in the three
generations of Avice Caro, "the artist in him . . . consumed
the wooer" (p. 66).

The distinction between the world of fact and the world
of fancy is constantly emphasized by the narrator:

Nothing could less express the meaning his recent news
had for him than a statement of its facts. [p. 73]

[Soon] the Beloved . . . informed a personality which,
while enrapturing his soul, simultaneously shocked his
intellect. [p. 91].

Trapped within his own dreams and in search of himself,
Pierston may be aware of his condition while remaining
incapable of altering it. He can only push on in the one
direction open to him: "Now he could be mad with method,
knowing it to be madness" (p. 102)—a statement that perhaps defines Hardy's own course after prose, *The Dynasts.*
Again, there are parallels between the sculptor and his
creator:

he would not have stood where he did stand in the
ranks of the imaginative profession if he had not been
at the mercy of every haunting of the fancy that can
beset man. It was in his weaknesses as a citizen and a
national-unit that his strength lay as an artist, and he
felt it childish to complain of susceptibilities not only
innate but cultivated. [p. 101].

"The highest flights of the pen are mostly the excursions and revelations of souls unreconciled to life, while the natural tendency of a government would be to encourage acquiescence in life as it is" [*Life*, p. 240]

We recall Hardy's remark about Eustacia:

Thus we see her in a strange state of isolation. To have lost the godlike conceit that we may do what we will, and not to have acquired a homely zest for doing what we can, shows a grandeur of temper which cannot be objected to in the abstract, for it denotes a mind that, though disappointed, forswears compromise. But, if congenial to philosophy, it is apt to be dangerous to the commonwealth.

There is an unmistakable resemblance between Eustacia's twin acts of disrupting the community and unveiling Clym's wooden intellectualism, and Pierston's projective mental processes. As if to emphasize the subjective nature of the record of Pierston's history, Hardy reminds us that the natural features of the sculptor's native island "looked just the same as before" (p. 145) to the apparently objective eye of the narrator. Jocelyn's "desire" is contrasted with his "understanding" (p. 179), as the book furnishes yet another version of the novelist's own contraries. When Pierston's illness destroys his artistic faculties late in the novel, his social isolation, in Hardy's mind, is terminated; he is at last successful in marrying and in performing practical services to his native community.

But the real concern of *The Well-Beloved* helps us to define the movement of Hardy's novels even more clearly. The working recognition that the mind functions in a projective manner unifies the developments that our perspective has revealed in his fiction. Not only is an identity suggested between the fictive nature of art and the perceptive faculties in general—the true instability of community is made correspondingly apparent by such an equation. And yet there is a deeper conflict: both the community and the artist ground their values in an implicit oneness with the earth. Here, the initial contraries of the artist must be reinvoked. If the community rests on a foundation illusory to the rational eye, it is because the rational mentality is itself fragmented, unable even to know the experience of natural unity, and hence predisposed to condemn it as an illusion. The artist, on the other hand, laments the violation of unity by the perpetually restive intellect and attempts to destroy the infecting element. Because a self-consciously experienced oneness is an impossibility, the artist seeks to rediscover in the individual the involuntary, instinctual basis upon which even the most fragmented minds must stand. But in searching for the natural beneath the massive machinations of self-consciousness, the question of social origins is once more raised, though this time in a suspect form. Similarly, a realization of the repressive nature of society also reactivates the notion of a necessarily illusory community. The question finally remains an open one, posing most comprehensively as a problem of history.

In 1875, Hardy recorded some thoughts on style:

> Am more and more confirmed in an idea I have long held, as a matter of common sense, long before I thought of any old aphorism bearing on the subject: "Ars est celare artem" [art lies in concealing art]. The whole secret of a living style and the difference between it and a dead style, lies in not having too much style —being, in fact, a little careless, or rather seeming to be, here and there. It brings wonderful life into the writing. [*Life,* p. 105]

A detailed study of Hardy's style would reveal the increasing presence of two kinds of narrative voices as the novels develop. The stylistic ideal described above is invariably violated, especially in his later work. While he often writes so directly that we are hardly conscious of the narrator's presence, we have also noted his tendency toward gross conceptualization and philosophical asides. A similar duality is reflected in the tension between narrative methods.

In the mid-Victorian novel, "[j]udgment is controlled [and] meaning made clear through the conceptual framework established" by the author.[4] Hardy came into conflict with this assumption—most obviously in *Jude the Obscure* —but only in terms of the content of his novels. He could not follow out his insights in his method: he exhausted the cognitive conventions of a public world to proceed to a private, individual universe, though in the subject of his work alone. The need to extend his recognition into the realm of style and approach could not be satisfied, as we have seen in *Jude*. And even though he disavowed a community sensibility in terms of the content of his fiction, he retained a conscious belief in rational modes of thought to the extent that he continued to share a common set of cognitive assumptions structurally. For even though *The Well-Beloved* grants full recognition to the projective basis of mental functioning, the very technique of recognition maintains a distance between the discovery and the mode of its presentation to the reader.

While the subject of an artist's reveries is not controlled by his conscious mind, his methods of presenting his imaginative discoveries remain bound to his intellectual scrutiny. With Hardy, a dichotomy always existed between his intellectual side and his "churchy" layer. Thus, the limits that his conscious mind placed on his dramatic capacities was intensified by his inability to adjust style and structure to the subject of his fiction.

It was to his first love, poetry, that Hardy returned when he decided to stop writing novels. Critics who have traced a continuity between his late prose and his poetry invariably point only to the conceptual or philosophical aspects of the novels. They bypass entirely the driving force behind the evolving universe of his fiction. The kinds of phrasing

4. Garrett, *Scene and Symbol from George Eliot to James Joyce,* p. 30.

and tone they select from his prose are chosen because they suggest the diction and the perspective of his poetry. As we have suggested, these readers miss the irony and the implied distance between the human processes ongoing in the novels and the narrator's own deluded attempt to explain the drama that escapes even his understanding—for example, this view that sees the vision of *The Dynasts* prefigured in the novels:

> In *The Woodlanders* the Will appears as an implacable "Unfulfilled Intention," or "Cause," whose laws predestine human beings to suffer in the battle of life. A similar fatalism pervades *Tess of the D'Urbervilles,* where the power is felt by Tess to be "an immense sad soul," while Angel Clare sees it as an "unsympathetic First Cause." Finally, in *Jude the Obscure* (1895), the concept of the Immanent Will emerges clearly defined in the pantheistic meditations of Sue.[5]

The question of Hardy's "pessimism" seems, at this point, a wholly irrelevant matter. Those who first pasted that label upon his work during his lifetime no doubt suffered from the same shortsightedness that appears to characterize many writers on Hardy even today. His own reasons for discounting such a description probably help us to understand him as little as most of his critics and biographers do. He countered the charges of "pessimism" with an idea he termed "evolutionary meliorism," [6] a product of the same aspect of his mind that apparently blinded his intellect from understanding the nature of his own dramatic energy.

Once his early faith had been destroyed by a conversion to rationalism as a young man, Hardy released a stream of impulses in his novels that led him, with an inner logic, to the limits of his ability—perhaps even of his sanity— in *Jude the Obscure*. While his poetry may still contain an

5. Georg Roppen, *Evolution and Poetic Belief,* p. 302.
6. Cf. Hardy's introductory "Apology" to *Late Lyrics and Earlier, Collected Poems,* pp. 526–27.

inconsolable despair, the tension in his means of expression, "the ache of modernism," is at least reduced to a tolerable level in his verse. To find the set of concepts that correspond to Hardy's directing dramatic insights, one must look to Freud's generation—the generation that also gave birth to Joyce, who was to find a corresponding structural solution to the conflicts in Hardy's imagination in the fulfillment of his own youthful aims; and to D. H. Lawrence, who was to inherit and transform, perhaps more than any other writer of his time, the legacy of Hardy the novelist.

Selected Bibliography

Annan, Noel. *Leslie Stephen: His Thought and Character in Relation to His Time*. Cambridge, 1952.

Bush, Douglas. *Science and English Poetry*. New York, 1950.

Chew, Samuel C. *Thomas Hardy: Poet and Novelist*. New York, 1928.

Daiches, David. *The Novel and the Modern World*. Chicago, 1955.

Darwin, Charles. *Autobiography 1809–1882*. New York, 1969.

———. *The Foundations of the Origin of Species: Two Essays Written in 1842 and 1844*, edited by Francis Darwin. Cambridge, 1909.

———. *Journal of Researches (The Voyage of H.M.S. Beagle)*. New York, 1957.

———. *The Origin of Species*. 1st ed. Baltimore, 1968.

Davidson, Donald. *Still Rebels, Still Yankees, and Other Essays*. Baton Rouge, La., 1957.

Deacon, Lois, and Coleman, Terry. *Providence and Mr. Hardy*. London, 1966.

Eiseley, Loren. *Darwin's Century*. New York, 1961.

Freud, Sigmund. *The Standard Edition of the Complete Psychological Works of Sigmund Freud*. London, 1958.

Frye, Northrop. *A Study of English Romanticism*. New York, 1968.

Garrett, Peter K. *Scene and Symbol from George Eliot to James Joyce*. New Haven, 1969.

Guerard, Albert. *Thomas Hardy*. Norfolk, Conn., 1964.

Hardy, Thomas. *The Dynasts*. New York, 1931.

———. *The Short Stories of Thomas Hardy*. London, 1928.

Hedgcock, F. A. *Thomas Hardy: Penseur et Artiste*. Paris, 1911.

Himmelfarb, Gertrude. *Darwin and the Darwinian Revolution.* New York, 1962.

Holloway, John. *The Charted Mirror.* New York, 1962.

———. *The Victorian Sage.* Hamden, Conn., 1962.

Houghton, Walter E. *The Victorian Frame of Mind, 1830–1870.* New Haven, 1957.

Howe, Irving. *Thomas Hardy.* London, 1969.

Hughes, H. Stuart. *Consciousness and Society.* New York, 1958.

Hyman, Stanley Edgar. *The Tangled Bank: Darwin, Marx, Frazer, and Freud as Imaginative Writers.* New York, 1966.

Johnson, Lionel. *The Art of Thomas Hardy.* New York, 1965.

LaValley, Albert J., *Carlyle and the Idea of the Modern.* New Haven, 1968.

Lawrence, D. H. *Selected Literary Criticism,* edited by Anthony Beal. New York, 1969.

Lynd, Helen. *England in the Eighteen-Eighties.* New York, 1945.

Maitland, Frederic W. *The Life and Letters of Leslie Stephen.* London, 1906.

Miller, J. Hillis. *Thomas Hardy: Distance and Desire.* Cambridge, 1970.

Peckham, Morse. *Beyond the Tragic Vision: The Quest for Identity in the Nineteenth Century.* New York, 1962.

Purdy, Richard. *Thomas Hardy: A Bibliographical Study.* London, 1954.

Roppen, Georg. *Evolution and Poetic Belief.* New York, 1957.

Rutland, William R. *Thomas Hardy: A Study of His Writings and Their Background.* New York, 1962.

———. *Thomas Hardy.* London, 1938.

Stephen, Leslie. *Hours in a Library.* 3 vols. London, 1889.

Stevenson, Lionel. *Darwin Among the Poets.* Chicago, 1932.

Van Ghent, Dorothy. *The English Novel: Form and Function.* New York, 1961.

Weber, Carl J. *Hardy of Wessex: His Life and Literary Career.* Hamden, Conn., 1962.

Webster, Harvey Curtis. *On a Darkling Plain: The Art and Thought of Thomas Hardy.* Chicago, 1947.

Whitehead, Alfred North. *Science and the Modern World.* New York, 1969.

Willey, Basil. *Nineteenth Century Studies.* New York, 1966.

―――. *More Nineteenth Century Studies.* New York, 1966.

Zabel, Morton Dauwen. *Craft and Character in Modern Fiction.* New York, 1957.

Index